The Way
of the
Tortoise

The Way of the Tortoise

*Why You Have to Take
the Slow Lane to Get Ahead*

MATT LITTLE

**With a foreword by
Sir Andy Murray**

Michael O'Mara Books Limited

To Oscar

First published in Great Britain in 2021
by Michael O'Mara Books Limited
9 Lion Yard
Tremadoc Road
London SW4 7NQ

A CIP catalogue record for this book is available from the British Library.

Papers used by Michael O'Mara Books Limited are natural, recyclable products made from wood grown in sustainable forests. The manufacturing processes conform to the environmental regulations of the country of origin.

ISBN: 978-1-78929-260-2 in hardback print format
ISBN: 978-1-78929-332-6 in trade paperback print format
ISBN: 978-1-78929-273-2 in ebook format

1 2 3 4 5 6 7 8 9 10

www.mombooks.com

Designed and typeset by D23

Printed and bound by CPI Group (UK) Ltd, Croydon, CR0 4YY

CONTENTS

FOREWORD:
SIR ANDY MURRAY

Matt has been a part of my set up for over twelve years now, helping lead my performance support team and introducing cutting-edge technology and monitoring systems to my training. During that time, we've experienced plenty of highs and lows. In the demanding environment of world tennis, it is rare to see working relationships last more than a few years because of the daily stressors that are placed on players and support staff.

Players and their teams are typically together for at least thirty-five to forty weeks of the year, eating breakfast, lunch and dinner together as well as pushing each other on a daily basis to improve. But, as with anything in life, pressure will either make or break you and in terms of my relationships with my team, the former is true, even if we don't always feel that way.

Over the last few years, I've had a very tough time with injuries, captured in my recent Amazon documentary *Resurfacing*. It was a daily struggle for everyone involved, desperately trying to seek solutions. In order for a team to function, there has to be trust, patience and a willingness to put in the hard work and sacrifice that is all encompassing at this level. We all had to deal with pressure and many failures and setbacks before we finally saw some success.

Obviously, there is a high level of technical knowledge and skill required around each expert that I employ in my team, but soft skills and 'feel' are important for the different and dynamic situations that arose on an almost daily basis, be it in training, recovery or any aspect of the process for that matter. Matt has been a part of that journey and been a highly effective team member every step of the way. Indeed, part of the reason that I initially recruited Matt to help me with my fitness was down to the values he has.

Creating a fun environment along with interesting, varied sessions is also vital. As seen in the documentary, this can mean getting my support team involved in my training to spice things up a bit. Those lighter, funnier moments are important, and sometimes it's good to wind each other up a bit! After all, if I have to suffer sometimes, I want my team to suffer as well. This all links back to the repetitive nature of elite-level sport. Keeping the athlete and the team energized and focused while having a bit of fun was definitely important to me and the people around me, who have all worked with me for many years. And that is where my performance support team were crucial in helping me, through not just these recent tough times, but from the early days, too.

I know that Matt's career journey was a long, slow rise to reach the level that he is working at today, and that's not just as part of my team. Matt has been involved in elite-level tennis for over fifteen years, working with players and teams of all ages from the bottom to the very top of the game. Whether it's part of the Davis Cup team that won in 2015, or his work with junior players with the Lawn Tennis Association, Matt has given his all.

I know the level of commitment, honesty, loyalty and drive it has taken to get to where we are today. Matt and I push each other hard every day to be the best we can be, and it is those values and soft skills I mention that have played a big role in this.

INTRODUCTION:
MY JOURNEY TO THE TOP

I am a rare example of someone who knew exactly what he wanted to do for a living from the age of sixteen. I lived for playing sport. I grew up in a town called Sutton in the county of Surrey, which sits just outside of London. I had a pretty normal, suburban, middle-class upbringing. Just like many boys of my age in Sutton, I spent every weekend playing football out on the fields. My parents would barely see or even hear from me from Friday until Sunday evening, when I'd crash through the door just to get to bed in time for school the next day. By our mid-teens, my friends and I had discovered tennis, and we were already hanging out at our local tennis centre every minute we could find. We were captivated by the sport and its superstars like Boris Becker and Andre Agassi.

Even though I absolutely loved sport and considered myself to be pretty good, I now look back and realize I wasn't particularly talented. Certainly not at the level to make a living professionally. Little did I know, this would be my first Hare and Tortoise moment.

What do I mean by that? Well, let's start with that old fable, written by an ancient Greek called Aesop some 2,500 years ago. The story of the Hare and the Tortoise is well known throughout the Western world. It tells the tale of a Tortoise who becomes irritated when taunted by a Hare about his slow, lumbering movements and so he challenges the Hare to a race. The arrogant Hare accepts immediately.

Of course, the favourite for the race is the Hare, who gets off to such a flying start that he feels he can stop for a rest. When the Hare falls asleep through his complacency, he allows the Tortoise to overtake him and ultimately win the race. Aesop's key message is that victory isn't always to the swift! And here, then, lies the central message of this book.

When we are young, we have visions, dreams of the life we want to lead, of blazing a trail in our desired profession. My message to each and every one of you reading this book is that, no matter what your current skill level or present knowledge around that profession, it is absolutely possible to achieve your dreams.

In my view, there are two distinct routes to getting there: the fast, risky, direct track (Hare); and the slower, patient, meandering track (Tortoise). My focus is on the latter.

SLOW DOWN TO GET AHEAD

These days, a lot of people at entry level in their careers want a fast track to their dream job. Young coaches regularly ask me, 'How can I get to work with a top tennis player?' The reality for most of them is that a route similar to the one that I have chosen is far more likely to get them to where they want to be. It's going to take ten years of sacrifice, total commitment and sleepless nights to even arrive at a place where they are ready to do the job. Then, once they start, they'll probably need another five years to become competent at that level.

You might imagine the reaction I get when I pass on this message. First, a look of baffled disappointment, followed by a verbal comeback that they'll get there much faster and prove me wrong. While I don't have a huge issue with this response, I've got a whole book's worth of time here to share my concerns about those who are looking for a fast-track route to success.

If you're a low-patience, high-intensity fast-tracker, you may want to skip the uncomfortable, the mundane and the unglamorous, but in doing so you'll inevitably miss out on so many rich experiences that will give you the solid foundations to become truly great at what you do. You might avoid what you see as the humdrum nature of slowly working your way to the top, but by racing on you'll accumulate some large gaps in your skill set that will let you down later on.

The slower route, the way of the Tortoise, not only gives you the time to take note of the finer aspects of your career when they come along, but also prepares you for the high-pressure, high-profile job when you get it. To reach that level, you will have been on a tough personal journey, gaining a broader base of experience, a more graduated exposure to pressure and more time to develop your own methodology.

So, for me, being a Tortoise is both a more gratifying approach and more likely to provide true, lasting success by giving you the necessary tools to be really good at your chosen profession. My gradual journey to success gave me the ability and stamina to turn my passion into a lifelong career and, I believe, taught me some valuable lessons that I'd be lost without.

In the opening chapters of this book, I'll be talking about the kinds of characteristics and values that we might associate with the Tortoise, from the core traits of loyalty, passion, positivity and generosity to a range of values that every Tortoise needs to work on and develop if they are to be successful.

I will also devote some time to looking at Hares and their very different set of attributes and values, such as impatience, impulsivity and overconfidence. This is not to say that such people cannot achieve success. Many Hares can be found leading industries and even countries, but success for Hares can often be short-lived, due to both their approach in attaining it and their behaviour once they have it. Although you're probably not a Hare yourself if you're reading this book, you'll certainly be familiar with them – making promises, talking up their achievements, winging it and moving at the speed of light. Doing anything, in fact, but keeping their head down.

MY PERSONAL TORTOISE RACE

My friends and I only really discovered tennis at the age of thirteen, when a local club opened and gave priority access to junior players. While visiting with school, we all absolutely loved the place and afterwards spent a vast amount of our time there, all becoming competent players pretty quickly. We idolized the professional players we saw on TV, obsessively studying their matches and sleeping on the pavement outside Wimbledon every summer to buy tickets and see them in action.

Looking back, I now realize that none of us stood any chance whatsoever of becoming professionals. The players we idolized, and even many of our peers in local competitions, had been playing a lot of tennis from an incredibly young age. And here we were, only just getting to grips with the sport in our early teens and aspiring to compete professionally. Unbeknown to us, we were thinking like Hares.

There's an entire debate about skill levels, talent, athletic ability and competitive spirit to be had here. Had any of us possessed a fair measure of each, it could have played a significant role in our dreams of turning pro. But, knowing what I know now, I realize how rare Hares are in elite sport. To make it to the top of most sports, you need to have been a Tortoise from a young age, to have been training your whole life. As Daniel Coyle writes about in his book *The Talent Code*, 'making it' in sport can often be attributed to the simple fact that you happen to live near a great coach, coaching programme or centre of excellence, which draws you in and nurtures you well – if only our tennis centre had opened ten years earlier! However, this is no tale of woe. I absolutely loved every minute of my sporting childhood. When I quickly realized I wasn't at the level to make any money playing tennis, I still knew I'd make a career out of it another way.

I went on to study with the specific aim of becoming an expert in the physical training aspect of the game. I have to say that my academic qualifications were not optimal for working at the highest level of professional sport. I flunked science at school, which meant that Sports Science degrees were unavailable to me. Yet, I made the best of it, going on to study Leisure Management – half business, half sports science.

Unsurprisingly, leaving university with this degree did not throw open any doors in the world of elite sport. But I volunteered, pestered, observed and travelled to wherever the top athletes trained to network and learn. I worked for years in entry-level gym positions, cleaning machines and folding towels, but at the same time taking it all in and learning from the top trainers whom I encountered, who worked with professional tennis players.

Eventually (an important Tortoise word), I earned an opportunity to work with national-level players at the tennis centre where I'd first begun to play. Here, I spent my time figuring out what worked and what didn't, and making plenty of mistakes.

What next? Well, I plateaued, that's what. My work with the players became stagnant. I felt like I'd hit a ceiling of opportunity at the centre. I sensed I could easily let the next ten years of my life drift by in that job without getting anywhere.

One evening, I found myself watching the movie *American Beauty*. The lead character, Lester Burnham, becomes bored with his dead-end existence, so he reinvents himself as an edgy, pot-smoking go-getter. Sitting there, watching Lester, I had an epiphany – and not about smoking pot. It suddenly hit home with some force that I only had one life and I'd better go out, take a few risks and find a new direction. Only I could move my life in the way I wanted it to go.

That night, I took a dramatic decision to leave everything I knew behind and travel halfway around the globe to Australia. I wanted to gain exposure to some world-leading coaches and tennis players. With its long, sunny seasons and great outdoors culture, Australia had an exceptional tennis pedigree and many professionals, both upcoming and established, had opted to live and train there, attracted by the facilities and the skilled trainers who had also flocked down under.

A few days later, I quit my job and spent the next month preparing for my trip. I wrote to every Australian state tennis centre, as well as the Institute of Sport, again and again, asking to volunteer or simply to be allowed to observe their practices.

Although I hassled and hustled my way in, people in these Australian institutions were fantastic to me. Not only did I succeed in finding paid work – with Western Australia's state tennis coach, Mark Taylor – I gained a huge amount of knowledge and experience. Arriving in Australia with just a few hundred pounds and a credit card, I managed to make my limited funds stretch for an entire year, working other paid jobs in between volunteering.

One of the stories that highlights my ambition to make a success of the trip was when I arrived in Perth and went to meet Mark Taylor, one of the people I'd been pestering. We hit it off very quickly and, as luck would have it, he needed some extra cover to fitness-train the kids on his programme. I began immediately and enjoyed a few months working at the State Tennis Centre in Western Australia. Mark was very good at his job and was soon headhunted for a bigger role over in Sydney, leaving me back in Perth with dwindling work.

A few weeks after Mark had begun his new job in Sydney, he opened his front door to find me standing there with my backpack. I thought he was the answer to all my questions about where my life was going next, and I hassled him for more work. Putting a good meal inside me and giving me a night on his couch, he managed to bundle me out of his house the next day and get on with his life!

As if by fate, when I returned home after my year of discovery in Australia, I got a call from Mark, who had since moved to the UK and begun working with elite British juniors for the Lawn Tennis Association at the University of Loughborough. It seemed he had forgiven me for doorstepping him, and he needed a fitness trainer.

So, there I was, back on his couch once more. I expect he was pretty relieved when I moved into alternative accommodation the next day. Several years down the line, we still joke that I'll forever be his stalker. That said, I learned later that being a Tortoise is also about networking and keeping in touch with people you meet along the way.

THE IMAGINARY FINISH LINE

A five-year journey of constant high effort, volunteering and working in low-profile, poorly paid jobs had resulted in my first entry-level job in Junior High Performance with Mark. I was finally working with international-grade junior tennis players. I thought I had made it. I thought I had learned all I needed to learn. I thought I was ready. I couldn't have been more wrong. I was about to spend the next five years on the world's steepest learning curve.

My boss at Loughborough University was Leighton Alfred, one of the best coaches I've ever met. Under his passionate guidance, I discovered what it was truly like to be on the edge of elite sport. I learned the right attitude, work ethic and behaviours, all through making mistake after mistake, then dusting myself off and going back in with the right mindset the following day.

Back then, in 2002, I had no idea what the tennis world had in store for me. I was sharing an apartment with my best friend, Iain Hughes, who was also based at the academy in Loughborough. Once a week, we'd go to McDonald's for breakfast and fantasize about working with the best players in the world, if only we could get the chance. Ten years later, we would both end up being employed on the professional tour: Iain with Elina Svitolina, who had established herself in the top twenty of the women's WTA tour, and me with the then world number three, Andy Murray. Today, we still pinch ourselves and use those breakfast conversations as a constant reminder of how things have turned out for us both.

After five years of cutting my teeth at Loughborough, a position became available at the National Tennis Centre (NTC), which gave me the opportunity to work with Britain's best professionals competing on the world stage at that time – Jamie Baker, Laura Robson, Ross Hutchins and Lee Childs, to name but a few. This was a huge deal for me. In the summer of 2007, I also struck up a good working relationship with Jamie Murray.

A few months earlier, while in the gym at the NTC one evening, I walked into the cardio area and came across an exhausted Andy Murray who was sitting on the floor. At the time, Andy was just twenty years old and had been competing in Grand Slams for two years, having reached the fourth rounds at Wimbledon, the US Open and the Australian Open. The small world of British tennis didn't have many top stars at this time, so Andy was acknowledged as a big fish. It was already clear that he was exceptional and on his way to achieving great things in the sport. This particular evening, he'd just been on the treadmill and looked as though he had pushed himself to the limit (a trait I was destined to witness on a constant basis). Later on in this book, I'll be talking about developing 'feel' for the moment. Meeting Andy by accident like this is my first good example of 'feel'.

By then, I had a decent amount of experience with elite players under my belt. I simply walked up to Andy, introduced myself and told him that if there was anything he ever needed help with in the gym he was to give me a shout. I then left him to it and walked out of the room.

If you asked Andy, I doubt he'd even remember this encounter. Which was exactly how I'd intended it to be. A less experienced, more overzealous me would have loved to have made that moment 'my time to shine' by telling Andy all about myself and asking him lots of deep, penetrating questions about his training methods and game, all with the aim of promoting myself. Had I done that, Andy would certainly have recalled the conversation, but for all the wrong reasons. It's unlikely he'd ever have wanted to work with me. Instead, I'd used the Tortoise strategy, hoping that taking a longer, subtler approach to getting to know an influential player like him would be by far the best approach. If that meant I didn't make a connection with him, then I would rather that outcome than the potentially negative one that can result from being too pushy.

As it happened, I was working with Andy's brother Jamie when he won the Wimbledon mixed doubles final in 2007. I went to an exclusive Japanese restaurant in London for dinner with him, Andy and their agent Patricio Apey. The boys even got 'papped' in my Toyota Corolla leaving the restaurant – a Hollywood moment, if ever I'd had one. When I saw Andy at the fiftieth birthday party of coach Nigel Sears (his future father-in-law) a few months later, we sat and bantered for several hours. Andy even asked me to take him for a training session the following week. During the workout, I was so pumped and overenthusiastic that Andy spent most of the time laughing at me. But he must've got something out of it. Some weeks later, he asked me to become a part of what is now known as Team Murray and I embarked on a decade-long journey, witnessing his rise to become world number one.

WORKING WITH TEAM MURRAY

Nervous wreck. That was me the evening before I left for Miami on my first trip to join a successful group of established coaches and physiotherapists – including Jez Green, Miles Maclagan, Andy Ireland and Louis Cayer – for our initial Team Murray training block.

I sat down to dinner with my old mate Mark Taylor. With him was physio Mark Bender, whom I knew pretty well already and who would in fact join the team himself a few years later. 'Just be yourself, work hard, keep your head down and try your best,' was the resounding advice from the guys that night. I tried to heed it, but after arriving in the States a ball of boundless energy and enthusiasm, I found that my lack of experience at that level made me the butt of the typical tennis banter for the next five years. What did I expect? I was starting at the bottom rung among these experienced coaches. Nonetheless, I still had their respect and was only too glad of the opportunity. I worked alongside the team and did everything I could to help create the best possible environment for Andy.

Once again, my learning curve was almost vertical. I spent a lot of time observing my teammates' interactions with Andy, the other tour-level players, coaches, agents and such. I definitely made many mistakes, but I tried not to repeat them. I had taken the Tortoise route to reaching this stage and so, even though every new level presented different challenges, my past experience gave me a solid enough grounding to meet them head on. Without that, I shudder to think how out of my depth I would have been when the team faced its biggest challenge in 2014, when Andy's tennis coach Ivan Lendl left and Amélie Mauresmo began settling into the role. As you can imagine, such a high-profile change of coach brought turmoil along with it. Andy had won his first two Grand Slams with Lendl, as well as a gold medal at the 2012 London Olympics.

After seven years as part of Team Murray, I'd slowly gained knowledge and proficiency at the very highest level of the sport. Accomplished and confident, I was now ready and able to lead. Unfortunately, on Lendl's departure, the complexion of the team changed as some other members moved on. As a result, I went from being one of the least experienced team members to the most experienced. I had stayed the course. Now, I could essentially marshal Andy's support team and help to steady the ship in rough waters.

When I look back at a decade of work with Andy, the Tortoise approach is apparent in every step I took to reach where I am today. It took me five years to feel competent and a further two years to be given greater levels of trust and responsibility. Any sooner and I wouldn't have been ready. I wouldn't have made enough mistakes or learned enough lessons. Using career stage classifications in my career that we'll apply later on in the book, my journey looks something like this:

PRE-ENTRY LEVEL: MY EARLY VOLUNTEERING DAYS

- learning training exercises for tennis players;

- refining my own style of comprehension from methodologies gained from mentors;

- learning how to interact with national-level athletes, their parents and coaches;

- travelling in Australia, developing independent thinking, self-responsibility and determination;

- gaining exposure to the very best coaches and athletes training in their environment, absorbing their intensity and attention to detail;

- making lifelong connections;

- showing future employers I was different and had drive, ambition and commitment.

ENTRY LEVEL: MY LOUGHBOROUGH YEARS

- understanding how little I knew!

- discovering how to handle the edgy world of international sport and still stand on my own two feet;

- cutting my teeth and testing my methodologies under intense scrutiny;

- starting to develop my 'feel' around the best players and coaches in the country.

EXPERT LEVEL: MY NATIONAL TENNIS CENTRE EXPERIENCE

- getting exposure to senior players and their coaches;

- taking my communication skills and confidence in backing my philosophy to new levels;

- being given positions of responsibility and management over other strength and conditioning coaches;

- accepting new challenges, forcing me to develop new skills.

INFLUENCER LEVEL: LEADING THE SUPPORT TEAM FOR ANDY MURRAY

- using my communication skills to work with top players and coaches;

- knowing and trusting my methodology;

- bringing to bear people-management skills and experience to think independently;

- still making mistakes, but far fewer than I would have without twenty years of experience behind me.

At pre-entry level, these were vitally important, formative lessons, not to be taken for granted. Those experiences at entry level were the making of me. At expert level, the mistakes I could get away with at lower levels were no longer tolerable. By the time I had started leading the support team for Andy Murray at influencer level, I was finally ready.

While the details of my journey may not align with your own, I do think it's important to examine each step and its significance. Too often, we look at those who have achieved without really appreciating exactly how they got there. Even though I wasn't aware of it at the time, every step of my long road to the top was vital to my continuing success. I'm convinced that so many people can benefit from treading this path and taking the slow lane to their own development. Time and time again throughout my life, I've seen that the way of the Tortoise is the only route to true, lasting success.

FROM THEORY TO METHODOLOGY AND SOFT SKILLS

At the first two levels, you learn how to ply your trade, but what does that really mean? For me, it's two things. Firstly, you form key values that define who you are and how you will respond to the situations that life throws at you. Secondly, you develop skills, learning the right theory to support the methodology that gets you the best results. Then, you need further abilities to implement this methodology in your own unique style.

By far the most standout skills I learned, those that would enable me to navigate my way to working with the best tennis player in the world and stay in that role, were soft skills. Soft skills apply to all areas of your working life and your personal life. They are the emotional intelligence and mental attitude required to generate success. I believe this is an area that is very much overlooked in the education provided by schools, universities and training courses.

Let's first contrast these with the hard skills that most of us will be more familiar with. In this day and age, hard skills have never been so easy to acquire, especially through study and the incredible resources available on the internet. How to hit a ball, how to breathe, how to recover. Understanding the application of this knowledge is, of course, a journey you must take. And, naturally, a few people are better at this than most. Essentially, however, upskilling is just the click of a button away and this is where most young professionals invest much of their time and energy. Much of this is good – these hard skills are a key part of the job. But, the aspect of how to be, or behave, in that job is often disregarded.

We all want to live happier, more successful lives. Which is why the soft skills that I focus on in this book are far more essential than courses on time management or problem solving. They are about emotional intelligence. The consistent behaviours you display. The interpersonal relationships you create. They are about your awareness of other people's perception of you. My experiences have shown me that you are far more likely to get ahead if you take the time to hone these skills than if you don't.

'You must get along to go along' is a phrase that may be familiar to many. But does this mean you must be a sycophant, a brown-noser, a doormat? Definitely not. Indeed, being headstrong, mentally tough and having clear views would be key traits in any successful person. But I believe that subtlety in your approach, and knowing the right time and context in which to display these characteristics, can be more effective and make you more endearing to co-workers.

Applying these skills also depends on your position on the ladder of success in your given field of expertise. The soft skills of an entry-level practitioner are quite different to those of a middle manager. But the fundamentals remain the same – the way you address other colleagues, how you carry yourself in your work environment, all have an impact. Having a feel for who you are and the level you are at is crucial. If you aren't aware of these things, someone higher up the chain will soon remind you.

For shooting stars, fast risers or those whose hard skills are incredibly strong, many of these soft skills may not seem necessary. Hares tend to set their own rules and blaze their own trail. These are the supremely talented, outrageously confident or just the plain bullish among us. Their work colleagues may put up with this behaviour because these individuals are too valuable to the organization to lose. But steamrollering people's feelings by being arrogant, forceful or abrasive requires the Hare to be constantly correct or successful. The minute a Hare makes a bad call or a mistake, just watch how quickly they fall from grace among colleagues.

Starting to think about your behaviours and your mindset can have a big impact on your effectiveness, as well as your perspective about your future. If you follow my advice as I take you through your potential career journey, you will not only reach your desired destination, but you will also have a smoother ride along the way. I hope that the experience and knowledge I'm passing on in this book will encourage you to follow the way of the Tortoise and take the time to excel in soft skills as you patiently build a successful career. It's not how to *do* but how to *be* that makes the difference.

HOW TO GET THE BEST OUT OF THIS BOOK

I'm not going to focus on the hard skills of your chosen profession, but rather on the consistent behaviours you display, your awareness and the interpersonal relationships you create. By taking on board the lessons from the Tortoise approach detailed within these pages, my hope is that you can use them to:

- develop processes that align with your unique vision and values.

- establish new daily habits that shape a positive mindset.

- seek out the challenges that propel you forward.

- feel confident in your ability to overcome obstacles and enjoy your successes.

Split into two parts, the book firstly sets out the difference between the Tortoise and the Hare in the race to succeed in life. We will look at what makes a Hare tick, and the pros and cons of rushing through life chasing instant success. I'll compare this to the way of the Tortoise and highlight the true value and worth of the slow lane, where people take their time while making mistakes and gaining the experience that makes all the difference down the line. You'll learn about the basic characteristics that identify a Tortoise. More importantly, you'll encounter the real values that are essential to success as a Tortoise in your chosen career.

Before you get into the right kind of training for the Tortoise you need to become, you'll take the Tortoise Test at the end of Part One. It's definitely worth finding out what kind of development you require to be the best Tortoise possible. You'll be able to tie the areas in which you're lacking directly into the relevant drills and exercises of Part Two. Armed with knowledge about the way of the Tortoise, Part Two will help you to progress towards Tortoise Boot Camp, a short-duration mindset week that will set you up for longer-term development.

With its practical advice, tips and skills practice, Part Two will be about acquiring the soft skills you'll need for career progression. You'll learn how to use and sharpen these abilities to transform yourself into the powerful, successful Tortoise you've always wanted to be. You'll get to understand the difference between emotional intelligence and soft skills, and there's an empathy exercise to develop that all-important sense of 'feel'. You'll also have the opportunity to work on your judgement, efficiency and understanding of others.

The longest chapter in this book, Chapter Five, details a diverse range of practical exercises to help you to think about how to deal effectively with pressure and failure, as well as success. We'll also look at learning to take care of yourself, your family and loved ones when the pressure is on at work.

But none of this will be much use to you unless you work out along the way how to make connections that count. We'll tackle one of the major challenges facing aspirational individuals: how to get your ideas and concepts across to those who have the authority or financial power to implement them. I'll share with you my buy-in matrix – a great tool for thinking about how to influence people at different levels with your ideas, assessing the likelihood of success and required effort. I hope through all these chapters you'll both learn from my mistakes as well as gain inspiration from my successes. Are you ready to follow the way of the Tortoise?

Part One

TORTOISE
BEATS HARE

1

WHY THE TORTOISE WINS THE RACE

There's a good chance that you either know a Hare or you've encountered one at some point in your career. Perhaps you're thinking of that team member who isn't afraid to offer their opinion at any given opportunity, whether it's informed or not? Or the colleague who will do whatever it takes to get ahead. The audaciousness of Hares often helps them to progress quickly in their respective organizations. Perhaps you recognize your boss or manager as a Hare? Such Hares may even enjoy the fear that their strong personality creates around them.

But, there are several downsides to their approach. Firstly, strong and aggressive personalities can alienate co-workers, creating a very lonely place for the Hare and making effective teamwork difficult. Secondly, an overly aggressive leader can stifle creativity and discourage people from speaking up. Sooner or later, colleagues will put their foot down and refuse to be treated that way, resulting in a dysfunctional working environment. And perhaps most importantly, the Hare takes a 'just enough' approach to winning, doing what's required to stay in front, rather than realizing their full potential.

It is also often impossible for a Hare to maintain their

high level of intensity for long periods of time, leading to fleeting success for many of them. For a Hare's co-workers, being around such an intense person for a sustained period can be a very tough task, hence a Hare's high turnover of jobs. Even if they stay in the same company, Hares can find themselves being moved around within it as managers and colleagues struggle to cope with them.

But this isn't to say that the savvier Tortoise gets ahead because of the flaws in the Hare's approach. Tortoises win not only by avoiding the mistakes of the Hares, but because they have their own key traits that help them to ultimately succeed.

TORTOISE TRAITS

In the next chapter we'll dig deeper into the finer details of Tortoise behaviour and the different Tortoise approaches, but let's first look at the four key characteristics that give Tortoises a competitive edge.

LOYALTY

When employers consider the many facets of an employee's character, one significant trait that they look for is loyalty. In the competitive world of elite sport or business, this is an all-too-rare commodity, making it all the more important to display.

It can be difficult to be honest about loyalty. Who among us could say we'd stick with a person, team or company through thick and thin, come rain or shine, on every occasion? But if our intention is to do that, it's a pretty good start for Tortoise development. I know the people in my own life who would do this for me. I also know exactly for whom I would be prepared to do this. The biggest decision is picking who and what you will be loyal to.

It is often said in the world of business that you should never be in the same job for more than three or four years, and that the only way to move forward at any pace is to seek a new opportunity. But it used to be commonplace to work for the same employer your entire life without question and I think we can still learn from this today. If your job and company are right for you, there's a lot to be gained by sticking with them.

An example that stands out for me is someone from my own industry of fitness – Planet Fitness, in fact. Chris Rondeau was appointed CEO of the gym chain in 2013 and, as I write this, the company is now worth around $6 billion, an incredible achievement. Rondeau went from working on the front desk of the very first gym in the chain way back in 1993, all the way to the top job almost thirty years later. He knew every little thing that made Planet Fitness tick, from the customer engagement at the gym entrance, to the cleaning and hygiene of each facility, before eventually helping the company open its franchises. He also changed the way Planet Fitness thought about its identity. Rather than selling the facilities to customers, Rondeau came up with the idea of selling the friendly atmosphere. This concept was a huge marketing hit and catapulted the chain to success. During his time at Planet Fitness, Rondeau will have survived several restructures, takeovers, ambitious Hares leapfrogging him up the ladder, junior colleagues who thought they knew better, new bosses treating him like he knew nothing and technological advancements that revolutionized the way the company did things. All of which, while stressful, will have only made him a stronger and more successful Tortoise in the long run.

Tortoise Loyalty

Rochester, New York State. 15 February 2006. High school basketball team Greece Athena are competing in their last game of the season with a very special addition to the playing roster. Jason McElwain is the student manager of the team, in charge of looking after the equipment and fetching the water. At 5'6" and autistic, he has never played a single minute for the side. As the game wears on, Greece Athena have built up a commanding lead. With four minutes and nineteen seconds left to play, coach Jim Johnson puts Jason into the game. The crowd goes wild. They have been chanting his name for the entire match. But no one could have predicted what would happen next. Jason receives the ball and misses the basket on his first two attempts. Then, becoming as 'hot as a pistol', he proceeds to make not one but six three-point shots and finally a two-point shot to boot. He scores twenty points in just over four minutes, the highest points-scorer in the game. At the final buzzer, the entire team sprints over to celebrate with Jason, along with the spectators, who also storm the court. This display of loyalty and affection by the coach, teammates and fellow students made worldwide news, catching the attention of President George W. Bush, who requested a meeting with Jason, ultimately admitting he 'wept, just like a lot of other people did'.

I understand that kind of loyalty. Working first for a sports governing body for twelve years, then for Andy Murray for over a decade, I couldn't have hoped for a better career. Of course, it's a two-way street and both of my long-term employers have shown me as much loyalty as I have to them. Hopefully, I repaid them by doing a good job. Not only did my loyalty to both pay off in a big way at the time, I like to think it will continue to do so for the rest of my life.

Fans of team sports around the world can all name a 'club legend', an exceptional player who stayed with that team for the majority of their career. Lionel Messi at Barcelona, Steven Gerrard at Liverpool FC, Ryan Giggs at Manchester United, not to mention Dan Marino and Tom Brady in the NFL (the United States' National Football League).

PASSION

Driven people feel incredibly strongly about their cause or mission. Their passion is the physical embodiment of that drive. You can tell when you're with someone who is motivated by ardour for what they do. Their energy, the conviction in their words, the 'fire in their belly'. They give you the feeling that everything that they are saying is not only true, but it is imperative that you believe in it, too.

For me, what passion looks and sounds like is personified by Italian-American basketball coach Jim Valvano. In the final game of the 1983 NCAA basketball championship, Valvano's college team, NC State, won the title with two seconds to go, causing a huge upset. I found some of his speeches online. Search them out yourself – they're brilliant to watch. One in particular stands out when he talks with infectious passion about his father and his mantra of 'You + Motivation = Success'.

I was also struck by a speech given in 2019 by the Brazilian women's football legend Marta, just after her side had been knocked out of the World Cup by France. Standing on the pitch, the thirty-three-year-old six-time world player of the year, who had scored in five consecutive World Cups without having won this most significant tournament, knew time was up on her career. Yet, after the final whistle, instead of bowing her head she chose to rally the younger players not only in her team but across the entire country. She called on them to follow in her generation's footsteps. 'We're asking for support. You have to cry at the beginning and smile at the end. It's about wanting more, it's about training more, it's about looking after yourself more, it's about being ready to play ninety minutes and then thirty minutes more.'

When watching rousing speeches like this, you wouldn't imagine a humble Tortoise behaving in this way, but you don't necessarily have to raise your voice or throw your arms about in order to speak with passion. When you think of drive, conviction and energy, these are precisely the traits that the Tortoise needed to win the race. They are just presented to the outside world differently. Any successful journey (or race) is fuelled by such zeal. In sport, business or anything else that you want to be successful at, a passionate attitude is something you just can't do without.

POSITIVITY

One of the lessons I've learned from time spent with mentors and high achievers is the power of a positive outlook. 'Stay positive!' is a message that rolls so easily off the tongue, but truly, when you're in a tough position and your back's against the wall, the effect of a strong character who sees the positives in the situation can be completely transformative.

Positivity and negativity are highly infectious. They can spread through a team, department or organization like wildfire. Those who simply refuse to moan about the negatives and convincingly affirm the positives can lead any team towards success. Convincing affirmation is certainly key here. If no one believes you, they will think you're simply in denial of the negatives.

If I have an injured athlete in front of me, I might say something like, 'I know you're disappointed about not being able to compete, but this will give us a chance to get that area much stronger than it was before, as well as giving you the opportunity to rest a little for the really important event in a few weeks' time. This injury could end up being a blessing in disguise!' This is significantly better than saying, 'That's too bad.'

Back in 1991, when basketballer Magic Johnson was at the peak of his powers and dominating the NBA (National Basketball Association), he held a press conference announcing that he was retiring after being diagnosed as HIV positive. Most people thought this was the end of the line for him and his career. At the time, the prognosis for HIV was very grim and read like a death sentence. But Johnson had a different view. He told the journalists present that he intended to live for a long time. He later said, 'It's funny, because the only time I think about HIV is when I have to take my medicine twice a day.' With this level of positive thinking, no wonder Johnson actually returned to the court to win a gold medal for the American 'Dream Team' in the 1992 Barcelona Olympics. Our potential for success is in our own hands if we remain hopeful and positive in our journey to get there.

GENEROSITY

Generosity is about giving – not necessarily money, however, or even good advice. What I'm really talking about here is generosity of spirit. A successful Tortoise needs to be able to give without the expectation of receiving.

Perhaps this isn't the most obvious trait of a winner, but being unconditionally kind to people can lay a positive groundwork that enables you to have much more productive working relationships. So often we think of those who are nice to people all the time as doormats, easily manipulated and placated. But being kind and being assertive are not mutually exclusive. Creating a rapport with a person before getting down to business is very effective. The way you frame things, your tone of voice and your body language mean that, even when you're saying something quite forcefully, it doesn't feel like a confrontation and therefore the other person is likely to be far more willing to accept your point of view. People who shout and scream may sometimes get what they want because they are intimidating and overbearing, but this way of operating can be energy sapping, create a negative atmosphere and is unlikely to be repeatable very often within the same environment.

We're all inspired when sportspeople show their human side in acts of generosity towards those less fortunate than themselves. Actually, there are far more of these deeds than we know about. I'm aware that Andy Murray has helped so many more charitable causes and individuals than he has been credited for in public. I think, being a discreet and private person, he quite likes it that way.

Actor Keanu Reeves has always struck me as a successful Tortoise. Even though he's worth a considerable amount of money, he is proud to be one of the only Hollywood stars without a mansion or bodyguards. He reportedly donated 70 per cent of his income from the movie *The Matrix* to leukaemia treatment hospitals (he'd grown up with a younger sister who had this condition). His generosity seems to be built on respect, humility, gratitude and appreciation: 'I was also raised to treat people exactly how I would like to be treated by others. It's called respect.' Author J. K. Rowling is another example of a Tortoise who has neither forgotten her values nor the lessons of life before fame. Despite being a single mother on welfare benefits when she began writing the Harry Potter novels, she became a billionaire through her determination to see her stories published. Tellingly, she lost her billionaire status in 2011 when she gave away approximately 16 per cent of her net worth (£100 million) to good causes and her own charitable trust.

SUCCESSFUL HARES ARE RARE

So, we know why loyalty, passion, positivity and generosity make the Tortoise a formidable competitor, but how do these measure up against the confident and risk-taking Hare?

Central to a Hare's ability to rise rapidly through the ranks is the capacity to learn and adapt at a much quicker rate than other people. This is linked to its high levels of intensity, as well as aptitude. The Hare's no-holds-barred approach means that it ploughs forward and makes mistakes faster than most, and therefore learns more swiftly than most. Hares tend to completely immerse themselves in their task in such a way that they accumulate knowledge rapidly. The more diligent or less complacent among them will read everything there is to read in a short space of time. They'll identify and get in touch with whichever experts they can and bleed everyone around them for information, arming themselves with the perceived know-how and attitude to excel in that area.

The disadvantage to this approach, of course, is that it takes time to master a subject. Even though the Hare may learn a great deal very quickly, there are bound to be gaps in this knowledge. More importantly, there will be gaps in their ability to apply this knowledge.

You might be thinking to yourself that many of the Hare characteristics – intensity, drive, ambition – sound quite attractive. Perhaps you imagine that highly talented individuals must naturally push themselves forward. But talent isn't quite as straightforward as we've previously thought. The idea of someone having a natural-born aptitude for things is much more tenuous than it once was. It's the old nature or nurture question, and there's a lot of evidence to suggest that the latter can be just as important, that practising a task in a deep enough way for a sustained period of time, and with the right person guiding you, is really the key to greatness.

And we have seen, too, that talent can be a double-edged sword. For those whose innate skills thrust them into the spotlight at a young age before they are ready to handle it, poor lifestyle choices and bad influences can ruin their chances of success. Being naturally better than your competition can enable you to trailblaze through the ranks of a given profession in a fraction of the time it takes others. On the other hand, superior ability can lead to complacency, a poor work ethic and a lack of urgency to build on your achievements.

The key lesson in the Hare and Tortoise fable is the clash of values between the two foes. I see these values playing out around me on a regular basis. Especially those at the start of a journey, be it a change of career or a desire to get fit. Getting fit and losing weight are very tangible objectives, and illustrate the two opposing methods to realizing your goals quite nicely. The Hare's typical approach to losing weight is to crash-diet, by completely changing what they eat, dramatically reducing calories and exercising like crazy.

Hare Risk-taking

Being confident and charismatic and being able to take risks sounds attractive, doesn't it. Perhaps you're dreaming of becoming the next Elon Musk. As one of the world's most prominent and successful innovators and entrepreneurs, Musk is notorious for taking huge risks on projects, having a world-changing impact and also experiencing failures. In his words, 'If something is important enough, you must do it. Even if the odds are not in your favour.' With this in mind, as with all Hares, Musk will fail occasionally. And when this happens, he will fail big. When he wins, however, as his net worth of $105 billion would suggest, he wins big. This kind of risk-taking can seem like the behaviour of a genius, but when the wrong call is made, suddenly the genius element seems less of a safe bet. The desire for great success at all costs can often backfire – sometimes the Hare will survive his impatience and ambition and come out on top, but, importantly, sometimes he won't. It's a precarious strategy.

The usual result is that the Hare does lose some weight initially, mostly due to fluid loss, rather than its aim of actually dropping body fat. However, the sudden nature of the adjustment that the Hare has made to its habits means this weight loss is unsustainable. In the end, the Hare regains the pounds it shed and is more likely to put on additional 'rebound' weight. The Hare has been starving hungry for weeks on end and its body retains the extra calories it's now taking on once more. The Hare has not made a long-term change to its physiology, lifestyle, relationship with food or, ultimately, its core behaviours.

It is widely accepted in the field of exercise and nutrition that the most sustainable way of losing weight is by making small adjustments to your diet and lifestyle on a weekly basis. What you are then modifying are habits and your psychological relationship with the food you eat. Those who lose just a few pounds each week are far more likely to keep the weight off because they have adapted their behaviour. Of course, this has the added benefit of being far easier to do compared to the Hare approach of shedding 6 lbs in a week, too. The Tortoise technique of gradually forming new habits and thinking about long-term goals in a sustainable way results in beneficial changes that can last a lifetime. So, if it's clearly better to lose weight the Tortoise way, then why aren't we all doing it? Answer this question and you've unlocked the reason why people become Hares, why society promotes being a Hare and my underlying motivation for writing this book!

It's important to note here that we should not always associate the Hare with failure. The Hare can be someone who achieves success at an abnormally rapid rate. Think of a fast riser in a company or industry, gaining promotion through the ranks of management and finding themselves in a senior position very quickly. Or, someone who creates a very successful start-up company, a newly popular politician or a *Britain's Got Talent* superstar who goes from nothing to huge success and sold-out tour dates. Clearly, Hares *can* achieve success. But few manage to handle it well and sustain it, and eventually end up crashing and burning.

So, what lessons are there in this message for those who are natural Hares? Are they all doomed to failure, never to achieve their dreams? Of course not. For a Hare to succeed, they need to have real resilience. They are either one of

Patience is the Key to Success

Impatience, like entitlement, can drive results but can also mean missed opportunities. While most of us are familiar with the saying that good things come to those who wait, in 1972 Stanford University psychologist Walter Mischel conducted a very revealing study to see whether children could be relied upon to follow this advice. The research looked at the theory of delayed gratification and compared children aged between three and six. The idea was simple: the children were left in a room and told that they could have a small reward (for example, a marshmallow) immediately or wait and get a larger reward (two marshmallows). Follow-up studies were conducted in the 1990s and the 2000s. The results showed that the children from the 2000s could wait one minute longer than those from the 1990s and two minutes longer than those from the 1970s. The reasoning behind this is thought to be twofold. Firstly, less draconian parenting, allowing for more self-responsibility, and secondly, earlier access to educational opportunities, which leads to greater cognitive function. It seems that even in the fast-paced modern world, young children can better understand the benefits of patience.

the very best in the world at what they do, so that people put up with them because they are too valuable to let go or, when they eventually crash and burn, they manage to pick themselves up, regroup and forge ahead, undeterred and as confident as ever. Resilience is a powerful survival skill, and if a Hare has enough, he might just be able to stay the course. But their risk-taking and lack of experience can often get them into situations that no amount of grit can bring them back from.

HOW TO SPOT A HARE

Hare behaviour can take different forms and achieve different outcomes. Whether it's in your place of work or in your personal life, you may well recognize these four distinctive Hare types.

THE SELF-DESTRUCTIVE HARE

A person who has genius-like qualities, but lacks the mental stability to control themselves or their environment. Like a shooting star, they eventually burn out, succumbing to the temptations of life outside their genius. This is the most common type of Hare in the music and arts industry. So much so that the '27 Club' has become a bit of a cultural phenomenon, highlighting the prominent actors, musicians or artists who have burnt out and died young, in this case at the age of twenty-seven.

THE FALSE HARE

False Hares are to be found in all walks of life. They are people who would have you believe that they are highly competent individuals, but as soon as you scratch the surface, you realize they are not. This is akin to a sports-car exterior with a go-cart engine under the bonnet. They have an inflated sense of self for their level of experience. This is often displayed by entry-level workers, who appear to be very confident in their own abilities without any relevant knowledge or understanding. This also applies to someone who has achieved wealth or fame purely through luck or timing, yet, once again, without the skill set; think of Lottery winners and reality-TV stars, or an inexperienced individual given a big opportunity by a relative or friend.

THE IMPACT HARE

A person who can be parachuted into a crisis situation and has the relevant qualities to handle it. Often ruthless and charismatic in the pursuit of a short-term win, be it a political campaign or business survival, this person doesn't really care what anyone but their paymaster thinks. Once their goal is quickly achieved, such individuals do not usually last long in their role.

THE SUSTAINER HARE

The most positive example of a Hare is the one who shoots to the top and manages to stay there, all down to their industry-leading hard skills and their ability to recover after failures – extremely rare in a Hare. The chance of finding successful Hares is certainly less likely in the world of business and commerce – opportunities are fewer and a hierarchy of experience usually qualifies others for promotion.

CASE STUDY: YOU CAN'T RUSH PERFECTION

In the wine industry, competition has developed between the countries and regions that have traditionally always made wine to a very high standard, and those emerging places around the world that are relatively new to this process.

Regions that have become famous for developing the world's best wines, such as Burgundy, the Loire Valley and Alsace in France, and Barolo and Veneto in Italy, have been producing wine for hundreds of years, and all of that knowledge goes into the winemaking process – centuries of trial and error regarding which grape grows best, in which area, which type of soil and climate combine to create the finest-tasting products, how and where is best to keep the wine once made, and even which type of wood to use in the barrels that store it. And each wine that they produce has been crafted by hand, from the people picking the grapes to the bottling and corking of the wine. As a result, they make far less wine than some of their newer competitors, but they achieve the best possible quality for that particular year's harvest.

Conversely, the regions of New World wine, which do not have many years of experience under their belts, must find a way to leapfrog the more traditional ways. In countries such as Chile, they are employing every piece of technology at their disposal, including satellite imagery, weather-predicting software, geological technology, micro-oxygenation of the wine and oak barrelling, in order to play catch-up with their Old World rivals. So much so that it can cost them up to £1 million per hectare to produce these New World wines. Many such wines are made in factories that utilize chemicals in the production procedure so as to cheapen and speed up the manufacturing process. As a result, they can make significantly greater quantities of wine than the Old World wineries. But at what cost to the quality, and does that really matter? In reality, much of the technology that is employed has worked and many New World wines are popular and taste fine. They are managing to put the right vines in the right place and harvest them correctly. But, in the opinion of most wine experts, although the

New World producers' wines are good, they are rarely ever great.

The elegance and style of a handcrafted wine is considered to be unrivalled and, in reality, great wine involves doing the minimum amount that you can to a fantastic grape. You can't cheat things like nature or the weather. It takes a lifetime in the vineyards and knowledge handed down from generation to generation, allowing the Tortoises of the Old World wineries to have the confidence to interfere very little with the process. Winemakers such as Trimbach in Alsace, Louis Michel & Fils – which produces world-famous Chablis – and Vietti in Italy have all snubbed modern and fashionable trends in winemaking for tried and tested methods, and their businesses have continued to flourish.

YOUR INNER HARE

Overconfidence and complacency are key traits of the Hare in Aesop's fable. As a successful Tortoise, I can reveal that there have been times in my life when I have displayed Hare-like behaviours. It is important to recognize these tendencies in ourselves and be mindful when our subconscious is leading us down this path, so that we can learn from the experience (positive or negative), understand the impact of our actions and attitude on others, and also ask ourselves, 'Did this behaviour result in a successful outcome?' There is a Hare in all of us to some extent.

When I was a younger fitness trainer, just starting out my work with lower-level, international junior tennis players, the opinion I had of myself was already somewhat higher than it should have been at the time. This became clear when the players I was working with became eligible to play at junior Wimbledon. I began to equate my own success and experience with these players as they advanced to the next level, and my inflated sense of my own achievements encouraged me to demand an 'all-access' pass from the event administrators. At Wimbledon, only the top coaches get into the practice courts, restaurant and changing areas. Imagine the battering my ego took when I was told I'd only be allowed a ticket to gain entry to the grounds and would not be allowed in areas near the players for their all-important tennis matches.

I was making the situation about me and my ego. Both desperately needed to be put in check. As so often happens when you get ahead of yourself, life brought me back down to Earth with a bump when I was refused. Even though it seems like a small issue all these years later, I was very put out at the time and made a fool of myself by complaining to anyone who would listen. Here, I was displaying the typical behaviours of a False Hare. Without possessing any of the substance, skills or the genuine success that some fast-rising stars actually have, I believed I was entitled to the rewards.

Another example of my own Hare-like behaviour is one that most people can probably relate to – driving. Most of the time, I'm very much a Tortoise behind the wheel. I drive slowly and considerately. I apologize for any mistakes I make. With no hesitation, I give way to other drivers wishing to go faster than me. Until I hit traffic, that is. Especially motorway traffic ... then my inner Hare leaps into the front seat. In the UK, we drive on the left-hand side of the road. On the motorway, you are generally expected to keep to the left also, unless you are overtaking, and you should not overtake another driver on the left-hand side. You always exit the motorway on the left, too. It's a pretty simple system.

When traffic jams strike, the Tortoises naturally bemoan their luck, but stay in their lane and wait to move. Not the Hares, however. They will either head straight to the lane on the right-hand side, in the expectation that this will flow the fastest, or start weaving their way in and out of any lane that moves – all in a desperate and impatient attempt to get ahead. The issue here is that, because the motorway exits to the left, it is very often the 'slow' lane on the left that flows more freely, not the fast lane on the right. And so, the Hare gets stuck in the fast lane. Of course, sometimes the weaver Hare behaviour pays off. You get ahead by switching lanes, but the impact it has on those around you is that, overall, the lanes slow down. You delay everyone else around you. On other occasions, your weaving does not get you ahead. You swing aggressively from one lane to the next, only to wind up alongside the very same cars you started next to, much to the joy of these drivers. Despite knowing this, I'm ashamed to admit that I am sometimes a weaver.

While Hares could not care less about their impact on others, they seem prepared to go through life in this stressful way. If we all stayed in the same lane, relaxed in the knowledge that we would all get to our destination quicker, wouldn't the hours we spend in traffic be more tolerable? Everyone has a basic 'type' and, inevitably, we sometimes revert to that type, especially when under pressure. Although I might display the odd (and unflattering) Hare tendency, however, I am fundamentally a Tortoise, and it is the Tortoise mindset that has shaped my path and led me to the success I've had.

THE AMBITIOUS TORTOISE

Certainly, in the fast-paced modern world, it feels as though to achieve any success in life you need an intensity and a strong desire to succeed, to get the edge on your peers. Yet my Tortoise approach is advocating a steady and therefore much longer path to achieve your goals. So, who has the most urgency? The Hare or the Tortoise? Everybody has a *desire* to succeed, albeit to different degrees. The Hare has the will to win, but actually suffers from a lack of *urgency*. It's faster, it assumes it will win, so it doesn't bother with a strategy for the race. The Hare just turns up as it always does, expectant and entitled.

The Tortoise, however, has urgency. Although it moves slowly, it is operating at 100 per cent. It is desperate to win the race and possesses the work ethic to follow through. Urgency and patience may feel like uneasy bedfellows, but they are both part of the Tortoise's essential toolkit.

Wherever you have competition in life, you have desire and urgency. For the rare, talented, standout Hare, competition certainly creates a desire to win, alongside the need to demonstrate its almost effortless superiority. On the other hand, the more common, less flamboyant Tortoise also wants to win, but it knows it will have to work harder than the opposition, prepare better and fight with greater intensity.

For all competitors in the sporting environment, whether Hare or Tortoise, no situation is more urgent than being behind in the scoreline. They are in a race against either the clock or the end of the competition. Fans of every sport will remember great comebacks and how they felt at the moment that the recovery began and gathered momentum. In the 2012 Ryder Cup golf tournament, the 'Miracle of Medinah' saw Europe recover a 10–6 deficit against the USA on the last day to win by 14½ points to 13½. In 1957, the football

Patient Urgency

A prime example of urgency meeting patience is Andy Murray's famed recovery from hip injury. The BBC documentary *Andy Murray: Resurfacing* showed viewers his painstaking two-year journey of rehabilitation and his ultimate return to top-class tennis. During this time, he experienced so many setbacks that he even considered quitting the sport. I have to say that watching Andy go through hour after hour of treatment and rehabilitative training, all the while being spurred on by a true urgency to get back to the match court as soon as possible, was one of the most impressive periods that I spent working with him – and there have been many. At the same time, there were stages in this process where Andy was told that he would not be able to even practise tennis for many months which, for someone who lives and breathes the sport, was a hammer blow. He had no choice but to exercise a great deal of patience throughout.

team I support, Charlton Athletic, won a match 7–6 against Huddersfield Town with only ten men on the pitch after coming back from 5–1 down with less than thirty minutes to play. In 2017, Super Bowl 51 saw Tom Brady lead the New England Patriots to a 34–28 victory after trailing 28–3 to the Atlanta Falcons in the third quarter. The attitude of these sportsmen demonstrates exactly what can be achieved with enough urgency. Against insurmountable odds, with the grains of sand emptying from the egg timer, almost any situation can be turned around with an urgent enough attitude. The Tortoise can beat the Hare.

WHY DOES THE TORTOISE WIN THE RACE?

- Tortoises are loyal, passionate, positive and generous, which leads them to be valued, driven and popular competitors – and ultimately winners.

- Hares are openly confident, charismatic individuals who can apply their audacious talents in spectacular short bursts, but their complacent strategies often lead to defeat.

- The Hare loves competition and has the desire to win, but usually underperforms, whereas the Tortoise loves it just as much and has the necessary urgency for ultimate victory.

- The Tortoise is more ambitious and driven than the more talented Hare because winning is harder to come by and takes more time, dedication and work.

2

WHAT MAKES YOU
A TORTOISE?

From a very early age, we push ourselves to walk, talk, read, write, learn, pass exams, excel at sport, look better, feel better, sound better and win. Before we even become aware of the competitive nature of society, we are thrust into competition. In many similar ways to Aesop's fable, we're all involved in some sort of race and are caught up in the belief that we must move fast or risk being left behind.

But it's *how* we go about winning that makes the difference. I think it's a fair assumption to make that if you're reading this book, you are a Tortoise already. But maybe you're not yet the successful Tortoise you're destined to become – the player who finally wins the sporting cup in their early thirties, the sergeant major who joined up as a teenage soldier, the school headmaster who has been teaching for forty years and seen it all. Such is the dedicated life of a Tortoise. A Hare may not have even read this far.

Look ahead and see yourself as the successful Tortoise of your future. You have dedicated your life to your trade. With that commitment comes automatic respect and trust. You've done your yards, earned your stripes, and now merit the accompanying kudos. You've been loyal to your cause – in itself its own reward.

Tortoises are far more common than Hares, so you'll have to work hard to earn your success. Understand that, like the Tortoise in the race, you'll be rising slowly. This is going to mean coming to terms with your gradual but inevitable progress. The Tortoise sees the Hare leaping ahead yet maintains a balanced and sure perspective all the way.

No matter what your profession – from charity volunteer to City stockbroker – the same rules apply. Your chosen way of life is one with purpose, challenge and steady progress. Speed is irrelevant, forward is forward. In the previous chapter we considered the four key characteristics that define a Tortoise. Now let's look a little more closely at the different types of Tortoise and see if you can recognize yourself.

WHICH TYPE OF TORTOISE ARE YOU?

As we discovered in the last chapter, not all Hares are the same, so it won't surprise you to learn that neither are Tortoises. Take a look at some Tortoise types below. You might feel very close to just one or be a mixture of all of them. No one kind is preferable to another, but it's important at this stage to think a little more about which one might be closest to describing you, as we'll use this to help hone your Tortoise skills later in the book.

NOBLE HERO

KEY CHARACTERISTICS

Works hard; keeps their head down; doesn't shout about their achievements; not much concerned with external acknowledgement.

STRENGTHS

A low-profile and low-ego paragon of humility.

DANGER SIGNS

Shows fortitude, but their low profile may lead to being overlooked for promotion, or not being promoted quickly enough in relation to their skill set or achievements, in favour of those who would self-publicize. Pay rises and bonuses are also often lower than they should be for this group. While unlikely to complain, if they are overlooked for too long, the Noble Hero will simply talk with their feet and leave the job, with honour, integrity and their head held high.

WHAT THEY NEED

Works better with a Tortoise for a manager who gives credit where it is due. Objective performance markers need to be in place for them to get the recognition they deserve.

LONG PLAYER

KEY CHARACTERISTICS

Believes in reliability, trustworthiness and playing the long game, and also understands that travelling for work comes at a price to interpersonal relationships. Their job is often a means to an end, or they are simply content with their lot in terms of their career, and they tend to prioritize personal goals over and above career goals.

STRENGTHS

Have chosen their path and are happy with it. They may live in the same town, stay at the same company and even be content at the same job level for their entire lives. They are simply not ones for change.

DANGER SIGNS

Can get set in their ways, or even stuck, should a move of job or location be required in times of restructure, forcing them to leave their comfort zone. Promotion would mean more stress, likely less time for their personal lives and the pay rise simply doesn't reflect these greater demands.

WHAT THEY NEED

Constant change is their worst nightmare, as they like routine. They need a manager who encourages them to accept some changes as part of life's inevitable challenges.

CASE STUDY: **THE LONG GAME**

An incredible example of sporting success that was achieved over many, many years is that of the Columbian weightlifter Óscar Figueroa. As a talented youngster, Figueroa was touted for Olympic glory and, in his first Olympic Games at Athens 2004, he almost medalled as a twenty-one-year-old. Figueroa then began working with an overbearing Bulgarian coach who pushed him to his limits. At the Beijing Olympics four years later, Figueroa didn't even manage to lift the bar off the ground. The press and other athletes accused him of being a rebel and not dedicated enough, but this turned out not to be the case. Something was wrong with the young Columbian. An MRI examination revealed that in fact he had a herniated disc in his neck and required a high-risk operation to put it right. Figueroa underwent surgery and bounced back to win silver at the London 2012 Olympic Games. But this wasn't enough for him, as Figueroa believed that he was capable of winning gold.

Disaster struck once again after London, however, when doctors discovered two more herniated discs, as well as arthritis in his lower back. Yet more risky surgery would be required to enable the athlete to compete again. By this stage, the weightlifter had been pushing his body to the limit for over fifteen years. The operation was due to take place in January 2016, with the Rio Olympics just seven months later in August. Recovery from major back surgery to lifting a gold-medal-winning weight seemed impossible. But Figueroa trained harder than ever and pushed himself to the brink yet again, finally managing to win a much-coveted gold at his fourth Olympic Games, twelve years after his first attempt. As he dropped the weights to the floor, the tears flowed. All the years of pain, hard training and overcoming so many obstacles overwhelmed him on stage in front of millions. Figueroa removed his shoes to signal his retirement and kissed the weights bar in one of the most emotional Olympic victories of all time.

STRESS BUSTER

KEY CHARACTERISTICS

Deals well with the stress and brashness of Hares; balances out the turmoil by providing an air of calm assuredness; absorbs the stress in a situation for it to move forward; acts as a cushion for chaos and uncertainty.

STRENGTHS

Their quiet, inner confidence. Without this type of character around them, most Hares would fail immediately.

DANGER SIGNS

They can deal with almost anything that the Hare throws at them with poise and grace, accepting that person and their behaviour as part of who they are and forging on regardless, refusing to take insult or exception, while others may look at this type of Tortoise and think 'Why do they put up with that? I'd never accept those behaviours and I would tell that person what I thought of them'.

WHAT THEY NEED

A manager who accepts their non-confrontational nature, allowing them to maintain their dignity with a more discreet kind of strength.

CASE STUDY: **LEADING FROM BEHIND**

For me, one of the most famous examples of a Stress Buster is Peter Taylor. He was the managerial assistant to the legendary football manager Brian Clough. The two formed one of the most celebrated and successful coaching partnerships that English football has ever seen, but it was their contrasting personalities which showcases this particular type of Tortoise.

Brian Clough was an extremely outspoken, brash, larger-than-life character (an archetypal Hare), with genius-like qualities that enabled him to get the best performances out of the players under his tutelage. By his side was the demure, softly spoken and camera-shy

Peter Taylor. His role was primarily to identify and nurture talented players to join the football club. As Clough would admit, 'Pete was the only bloke who could stick an arm around my shoulder and tell me – straightforwardly, mate to mate – that I was wrong, or right, or to shut up and just get on with my job.' He was the yin to Clough's yang. Playing this role so successfully clearly required a different kind of strength and a different set of values to that of his enigmatic colleague.

This dynamic duo took two clubs (Derby County and Nottingham Forest) from languishing in the Second Division to winning the First Division. An incredible feat to achieve once, never mind twice. On top of this, they also oversaw Nottingham Forest winning two consecutive European Cup finals in 1979 and 1980. Arguably one of the greatest managerial accomplishments in the history of the sport.

Tellingly, when the pair parted company, neither were anywhere near as successful and, tragically, they fell out towards the end of their careers. Their relationship highlights the need for there to be a balance of Hares and Tortoises in a team, and the powerful part the Stress Buster can play in an effective partnership.

TEAM CAPTAIN

KEY CHARACTERISTICS

Brings people together through effective mediating skills, making them very good leaders of teams; able to take different characters, with different opinions in different situations, and be the conduit for them to blend together; can get along with almost anybody, no matter how difficult, looking for the good in people and focusing on that.

STRENGTHS

Often referred to as 'the glue' that sticks people together. Possessing generosity and loyalty in abundance, they also combine low ego with humility while persisting in their task to create balance and equilibrium within groups of people, seeing the good in all.

DANGER SIGNS

Their position can be very lonely, as few others are likely to take on the role of managing hostile situations between two Hares or a Hare and a Tortoise, and then pitch this mediation at the right level to remedy the issue.

WHAT THEY NEED

Recognition as a team member who gets along with everyone and takes the time to resolve issues and organize social gatherings. They also need a manager who recognizes that they have a good relationship with all parties and can explain the team's perspective.

CASE STUDY: **CONNECTING WITH YOUR TEAM**

Born in England in 1966, the same year that the England football team won the World Cup, Jill Ellis grew up to become one of the most successful coaches that the game has ever seen.

As a football ambassador for the British government, her father, an ex-Royal Marine, coached football players of all ages and abilities, and Ellis would watch in awe from the sidelines. When the family moved to the US in the early eighties, women's soccer was flourishing and she went from watching to playing, achieving the accolade of third-team All-American, an honorific title given to outstanding amateur players. But it was her passion for coaching that really thrust her into the limelight.

One of the key things that she has learned from her father was his ability to connect with his players. Ellis became an incredibly successful US College team soccer coach, winning seven NCAA Women's College Cups (2003–2009) and six straight Pacific-10 Conference titles. But it is Ellis's more recent role as US Women's National Team Coach that made the world sit up and take notice. In a little over one year after her appointment, she led the team to victory in the 2015 World Cup, beating Japan 5-2 in the final.

She is impressive not only for the successes of her teams, but also because of the way she has managed strong characters and tricky situations along the way. She had the courage to overhaul the team after winning the World Cup, bringing in eleven new squad members and leaving several regulars out and, in 2017, survived a coup staged by several senior team members to get her fired. And, while preparing for the 2019 World Cup, her players issued a lawsuit against the US Soccer Federation, fighting for equal pay with their male counterparts. The media storm that followed would have been distraction enough for any team at any time, never mind during preparation for defending the biggest title in your sport. However, rather than distract or divide the team, with Ellis at the helm, this seemed to galvanize them. They ploughed through the tournament, once again without losing a single game. The closeness and connection of the team has been widely acknowledged as a key factor in their success.

Being the central figure for this team to look to for strength and advice, and allowing the strong characters in the dressing room to be themselves while introducing and nurturing new, young players is a true testament to Ellis as a team leader.

STEADY EDDIE

KEY CHARACTERISTICS

Works steadily, showing consistently high effort; tends not to stand out; is generally popular and a team player, and satisfies managers without blowing them away.

STRENGTHS

By far the most common type of Tortoise, they work their way up through the ranks of an industry or even within the same organization, showing an incredibly high degree of fortitude and consistently high effort.

DANGER SIGNS

Generally low-key in the way they come across to others. Hence, if they aren't seen to move with the times, keep up with developments and align themselves with the right colleagues driving change, they could get left behind for the more impressive (but combustible) Hare.

WHAT THEY NEED

A manager to encourage them to play two or three moves ahead. To be effective, they must accurately predict the course of the industry and prepare for this accordingly.

CASE STUDY: **THE TEAM PLAYER**

Born in 1923 in Germany, like many of his peers, Bert Trautmann became a member of the Hitler Youth as a child and later fought on the Eastern Front during the Second World War, earning himself five military medals, including the Iron Cross. After being captured by the British, at the end of the war Trautmann chose to live in England, where he began to play in goal for his local football club in Lancashire, St Helens Town, and became a reliable team member. He turned out to be a quite exceptional goalkeeper, and in 1949 he signed for Manchester City. Despite initial protests from the British public, Trautmann again proved his worth by going on to play 545 matches for the club.

This, however, is not exactly why Trautmann became a famous name in the history of sport. That came about when he played in the 1956 FA Cup Final against Birmingham City. With seventeen minutes left on the clock and with his team 3–1 in the lead, he was involved in a dangerous collision with one of the Birmingham players and sustained a serious neck injury. Ignoring the pain, he stayed on the pitch until the final whistle, making at least two match-winning saves for his team and being knocked out for a second time during one of them. He even attended the post-match meal, despite not being able to move his head. Three days later, an X-ray revealed he had broken his neck. Now, if that is not an example of a reliable, committed team player, then I don't know what is.

EMBRACE YOUR TRUE NATURE

By now, you might be starting to recognize similarities between my Tortoise descriptions and how you behave in your life. But you might also be wondering how you got to be this way in the first place, and how much of a role your inner Hare plays in your life, too.

While an environment or situation may influence a behaviour and bring different personality traits to the fore, I believe that, overall, people predominantly represent a type and, over the course of our lives, we consistently lean towards and achieve results from either one methodology or the other.

At the end of Part One, you'll take the Tortoise Test to determine exactly how much of a Tortoise you are and where you need to make the improvements that will bring you the success you want in business and in life. But it's important that we get to grips with your true nature now, before you test yourself. There are a few key areas that we can look at to give us a clearer picture of exactly who we are.

Personality clearly has a large role to play in who we are and our approach to life. When thinking of Hare-like personalities, an extroverted person would probably exhibit more Hare-related characteristics, whereas introverts may be more Tortoise-like. You can imagine the Hare being loud, brash and confident, with the Tortoise being quieter, measured and humble.

The next port of call would be **upbringing**. A parental influence that rewards risk-taking and allows for freedom of expression, assertiveness and even aggression could lead someone to becoming a Hare. Then there's the number of siblings a person has. Are they the oldest, middle or youngest child? Where do they sit in the pecking order for attention?

Such factors can make a child fight and push to be seen and heard. Alternatively, someone accustomed to receiving no attention might choose to stay quiet. Adversity in upbringing has been suggested as a theme among high achievers. On the one hand, this could give someone that extraordinary drive and cut-throat ambition to become a Hare. On the other, it might give a person the steely resolve to stay the course in a Tortoise-like fashion.

Past experience is highly influential in forming our adult behaviours. If you were forceful, assertive or even risk-taking as a youngster only to be punished for it, your future behaviour could develop differently. Getting your way and becoming successful, however, would only strengthen your early pattern. Similarly, if by being quiet or remaining in the background of situations you got to stay in your comfort zone, this may feel like the best place to be and become self-reinforcing behaviour in itself.

Finally, a person's **environment** can shape them powerfully, too. Growing up in a tough neighbourhood, with little money and few resources, could create a Hare's fight or a Tortoise's fortitude. Growing up in a comfortable environment can generate the sense of entitlement of a Hare, or the lack of confrontation in a Tortoise.

Some working environments – trading floors, political platforms or the stage – lend themselves to brash assertiveness, egotism and competitiveness. Others, such as healthcare, civil service or hospitality, seem more suitable for patience, trustworthiness and reliability.

If we're able to recognize where we've come from and the influences on our behaviour and personality, we can use this information to our advantage to seek the success that complements our true nature.

CASE STUDY: **A BORN FIGHTER**

For a truly inspiring example of how environments can shape people's perspectives and behaviours, look no further than the combat sports. Almost every successful fighter has a backstory of hardship that had to be overcome before they could achieve glory in the arena.

One such example that has inspired me more than any is that of mixed martial artist and UFC Women's Strawweight Champion, Rose Namajunas. 'Thug Rose' was raised in a very tough neighbourhood in Milwaukee, Wisconsin, as a first-generation American. Her parents were Lithuanian and her father, who suffered from schizophrenia, died when she was at the impressionable age of just sixteen. Not only did Namajunas have to deal with the daily conflict that came with living in a rough part of town, she has also indicated that she was sexually abused as a child. She never felt safe or comfortable even in her own home.

She became interested in Taekwondo at the age of five and soon progressed to other forms of martial art in high school, ultimately becoming a mixed martial artist and competing in the Ultimate Fighting Championship (UFC).

One of Namajunas' most notorious contests was as the underdog, in a title fight against Polish competitor Joanna Jędrzejczyk in 2017. The pre-fight build-up was extremely intense, with her opponent being overtly aggressive in the press conferences beforehand, making reference to Namajunas' upbringing and her resulting struggles with mental illness. All the while, the softly spoken American maintained her poise and dignity, even to the point of reciting the Lord's Prayer in the stare-down while Jędrzejczyk hurled physical and verbal abuse.

When the fight commenced, Namajunas delivered an incredible performance to knock out the Pole in the first round, causing one of the greatest upsets in the history of Mixed Martial Arts (MMA). The demeanour of both fighters made it feel almost biblical: the triumph of good over bad.

In her post-fight interview, Namajunas summed up her feelings and values, which were all the more incredible given everything that she had been through in her life and during the build-up to the fight: 'I just want to use my gift of martial arts to make this world a better place ... this belt don't mean nothing, man. Just be a good person, this [belt] is extra, this is awesome, but let's just give each other hugs and be nice. I know we fight but this is entertainment and afterwards it's nothing.' These words went viral on the internet and along with her win they made Namajunas an international star. She is now using her platform to raise awareness of mental health issues globally.

SET OUT YOUR OWN GOALS IN LIFE

Before you can get what you want from life, you have to know what it is you want. Comparing ourselves with others, competing with our peers and trying to 'keep up with the Joneses' are all concepts often portrayed as negative, but they needn't be seen that way. You just need to know what you want. True, if you chase such outcomes as ends in themselves, fulfilment will likely elude you. There's *always* someone better off than you, happier, earning more, driving a nicer car, going on better holidays. It's far better to say, 'My goal is to earn my first million', than 'I want to earn more than my teammate'. If your teammate gets a raise, or a promotion, that's a good thing – it should drive you to redouble your efforts to gain a promotion of your own. Competition is good – for individuals, for teams, for businesses. But we need to use it to help us to achieve our goals, not set them.

I will never forget walking around the Puerto Banús marina near Marbella, Spain. Blue skies, sparkling water, light bouncing off the quayside buildings. My gaze fell enviously upon a wealthy man, sitting on his beautiful yacht, who was looking out at the people watching him. At that moment, another much larger and far more expensive yacht reversed into the bay right next to him. The look on the man's face said it all and he soon disappeared into the bowels of his boat.

I'm sure we've all felt this way at some point in our lives. It's fair to assume that anyone who has a huge vessel moored in a glamorous location has achieved a certain level of financial wealth that most would aspire to. But, when an even bigger yacht pulls up alongside you, suddenly it doesn't feel like enough. If comparison with others is your yardstick for success, how can you ever be satisfied?

In the seemingly inescapable world of social media, comparisons have become even more dangerous. A common social media practice is to project an image to the world that life is perfect, and it's easy to feel that true happiness lies only in the accumulation of material wealth. For those caught in this sticky web, fame and fortune are the ultimate goals we wish to attain. What we don't tend to see or appreciate is the incredible sacrifice and effort it often takes to achieve these outcomes. Social media does not show the unglamorous hard work necessary along the way.

It's really important when you're thinking about your own attainment aims to set the right goals in the first place, independent of what other people are doing, and to only use their success as a motivator to go after your own. In the same way that when Apple released the iPhone, every top technology firm had to immediately raise its game and develop similar, if not better, products, you can use the drive and energy of others to boost your own.

When a sport has a dominant force like Roger Federer, Rafael Nadal or Serena Williams, journalists often ask other competitors if they wish they were born in a different era, so they didn't have to go up against them. While the question is put with an expectation of receiving a 'yes' in response, the professional's answer is invariably 'no'. Without those individuals setting such a high bar, the other players would not have reached the levels at which they currently play. Federer, Nadal and Williams make all the others better players.

WHAT MAKES YOU A TORTOISE?

- Your basic character means you behave with strong degrees of loyalty, positivity, passion and generosity – you're made that way.

- Unlike the Hare, you accept that speed is irrelevant, forward is forward.

- You don't shout about your achievements.

- You believe in reliability, trustworthiness and playing the long game at work and in life.

- You have an inner strength that you display through a calm air of assurance.

- You see the good in people and are often the glue that holds a group together.

- You're someone who is prepared to work their way up the ranks of your company or industry, showing an incredibly high degree of fortitude and putting in a consistently high level of effort.

3

HOW YOU BECOME A WINNING TORTOISE

We've looked at why the Tortoise wins the race and the key characteristics that define a Tortoise and its approach. But do you possess the right combination of Tortoise values? Do you have what it takes to be successful in your chosen career?

In this chapter, we're going to explore a set of eight Tortoise values that I believe are latent in every Tortoise. If we want to improve our chances of winning in life, we need to bring these attributes to the fore and develop them into powerful aspects of our approach to achieving our goals.

PATIENCE

If you had to work hard, leave family and friends behind, sacrifice your social life and endure possible failure time and time again, would you be able to stand it for a year? What about five years? Or ten? The success you seek, the dream you chase, is probably going to take you that long to reach. Can you wait for it?

In the modern age of instant gratification and real-time information, we've become impatient. We expect the latest news now, online deliveries tomorrow and overnight success. But if there's one thing that hasn't changed from one generation to the next, for the vast majority of successful people, their achievements were hard-fought and took time. For every billionaire start-up entrepreneur, there are millions of businesspeople with brilliant ideas who only see the fruits of their labour many years down the line.

PATIENCE WITH A GIVEN TASK OR GOAL

For a large part of the race in Aesop's fable, the Tortoise requires task-related patience. It has no idea how far behind it lags. It's getting beaten comfortably. Yet it still possesses the patience to stick with the task and see it through, no matter what. And it gets its just rewards!

PATIENCE WITH YOURSELF

Having patience with yourself calls for an even greater amount of control and regular practice. We tend to beat ourselves up for not succeeding as the world tells us we should. When acquiring new skills and breaking new ground, you won't get it right straight away. Allow these processes to take place without berating yourself. Give yourself time to achieve. The alternative is a very uncomfortable journey and an unfulfilled life.

PERSISTENCE

Have you ever begun a task, got frustrated and quit too soon, only to find out later that, if you'd stuck at it, you'd have experienced success? Like all successful individuals, the Tortoise in the race has a high degree of mental toughness. One of the key factors in this state of mind is persistence.

Overcoming Failure

As a heptathlete, Katarina Johnson-Thompson has to excel in seven different events, putting all kinds of pressures on different parts of her body. She is expected to be able to contest the 100-metre hurdles and the 200-metre sprint, launch the javelin, take the high jump, run 800 metres, throw the shot and make a long jump. The life of a heptathlete is about constantly improving your personal best in every event by incremental steps, while retaining your fitness for each and every one of them, as well as overcoming setbacks from injury.

After winning gold in the 2009 World Youth Championships, Johnson-Thompson missed the 2010 season with 'jumper's knee'. Climbing up the ranks ahead of her was Jessica Ennis, calendar girl of the London 2012 Olympics, and at the same home event nineteen-year-old Johnson-Thompson came thirteenth in a strong field. In 2015, she finished twenty-eighth in the World Championships in Beijing, after three foul attempts in the long jump, having been second after the first day's events behind Ennis. Believing in herself and determined to get over her earlier failures, Johnson-Thompson went on to win the heptathlon gold medal at the 2019 World Championships, breaking the British record with a score of 6,981 points and ranking her sixth on the all-time heptathlon lists.

PERSISTENCE LIKES A CHALLENGE

Persistence kicks in when we set ourselves tasks and encounter obstacles that we know we must get past. We find the determination to push on. We tell ourselves that getting through such a tough experience will be all the more gratifying.

PERSISTENCE NEVER QUITS

Every good parent has persisted in their task, raising their child to be the best they can be, despite setbacks, highs and lows, ill health and other stressors of daily life. People in every single job have bad days, weeks, months and quarters, but they don't quit. They resolve to go back the next day and try to do better. They fail continuously and persist until they succeed. Without persistence in any task, you are destined to fail.

PERSPECTIVE

Can you think of an activity or a goal where you played the long game? Did you keep at it? Did you have faith in yourself to succeed? I like listening to elite sportspeople after a tough victory, in which they have come from behind in the scoring to win. Their mindset is always fascinating. They refer to trusting in their tactics and their ability, knowing these would eventually ensure they prevailed. I find it so impressive that, under such immense pressure and scrutiny, they can have this sense of perspective and retain the presence of mind in the moment.

In November 2016, Andy Murray became the world number one tennis player. This feat is impressive enough in itself, but the statistics behind this achievement speak volumes about the persistence at the heart of his success.

At the age of twenty-nine, Andy was the second oldest player to debut at number one, behind thirty-year-old John Newcombe in 1974. He holds the record for the longest time between first becoming number two and becoming number one – over seven years. He had seven stints at number two and is tied by only two players in history that came so close, on so many occasions. When you put that into the context of the era in which Andy Murray has competed, with the likes of Roger Federer (who, at the time of writing, has twenty Grand Slam titles and been runner-up eleven times), Rafael Nadal (twenty Slams, eight times a runner-up) and Novak Djokovic (seventeen Slams, ten times runner-up), the word persistence barely covers it. Fittingly, Andy secured his number-one ranking with a match against Djokovic, the former world number one. It was the very last match of the season, and seven months earlier, Andy had been 8,725 world ranking points behind his Serbian rival. To give this some context, you receive 2,000 points for winning a Grand Slam event, so Andy had to make up a lot of ground between April and November 2016.

But Andy's single-minded daily approach to becoming the best he could be meant that when he got his chance he took it. All too many tennis players in his position would have lacked the faith that they could take that final step. Many would have stopped believing and lost motivation to keep putting in the extra work required. Andy's rewards felt all the sweeter because of his journey.

PERSPECTIVE PLAYS THE LONG GAME

No matter what the situation, being able to develop perspective is a very difficult skill to master. When things are going badly, thinking long-term is important to keep you

Having a Vision

The world of Formula One racing has never seen a story as incredible as that of the Austrian driver Niki Lauda. In 1976, Lauda began the season as world champion. He was at the very height of his powers and looking to back up his previous year's win with another championship-winning run. However, in the German GP in early August, Lauda suffered an horrific accident, with his car bursting into flames while the twenty-seven-year-old driver was still inside. He suffered severe burns to his head, lost most of his right ear and inhaled toxic smoke and gases from the wreckage which poisoned him. Lauda fell into a coma after the race and the prognosis was grim. The world of motor racing held its breath for the news about its champion. Incredibly, Lauda pulled through this terrible event and got back in his racing car just weeks after the accident, competing at the Italian GP in September. One can only imagine the mental strength it took him to go fast in a car again, never mind the physical pain of the helmet on such severe burns and repairing his battered and bruised body to deal with the uncomfortable rigours of racing once more. He missed just a handful of races during the 1976 season, and only lost the championship by a single point to British rival James Hunt. Lauda went on to drive for another nine incredible years, winning two more Formula One championships and, more importantly, the respect and adoration of the entire sporting fraternity. No matter how hard the challenges are that you face, with enough mental strength, determination and a vision, Lauda showed that you can control the controllables and turn any situation around.

motivated and to help you to see failure as a setback rather than the end of the road. Even when things are going well, it's just as crucial to avoid complacency.

I have been in the locker room immediately after huge wins and crushing losses. In both situations, the conversation very quickly turns to looking forward. Ultimately, playing the long game means you have a vision of where you want to get to, never wavering from this, regardless of short-term results. Stop at nothing to realize this vision!

FORTITUDE

What setbacks have occurred on your particular journey? Were you able to overcome this adversity? What did you discover in yourself during this challenge? It seems there's nothing we like more in our heroes than that good old quality called fortitude. It's perhaps a bit of an old-fashioned word today, but for me it captures that sense of guts, self-reliance and resilience that we've long admired.

FORTITUDE MEETS ADVERSITY

Any journey worth making, any career path, dream, relationship or goal will face adversity. The Tortoise encountered this when it was losing the race badly. It is in these exact moments – when you push on regardless and keep moving forward, despite the odds – that you will find out who you are.

FORTITUDE BUILDS SUCCESS

Fortitude means having the courage of your convictions and a firmness of purpose, especially in the face of adversity, and an unshakeable will to succeed even in the darkest of days. Focus on fortitude and you will develop a strength that turns you into the person who will ultimately be able to achieve anything you want.

Overcoming Adversity

American surfer Bethany Hamilton had a sponsorship deal with Rip Curl at the age of nine. At thirteen, she came second in the 2003 NSSA (National Scholastic Surfing Association) championship. Yet Hamilton knows all about adversity. Later that same year, while out surfing, she was attacked by a tiger shark which bit off her left arm just below the shoulder. Yet the pain and anguish of this event didn't stop her and, seemingly undaunted, she returned to the water just one month after the incident.

The following year, she competed once again in the NSSA Championship, collecting an ESPY Award for Best Comeback Athlete. Hamilton had taught herself to paddle even harder with one arm and kick harder with her feet. She used different tactics to other surfers to catch the waves at the right times and even had a handle fitted to her board. Her story was so inspiring that a film about her, *Soul Surfer*, was released in 2011.

In 2015, just three months after the birth of her first child, she competed in another professional surfing competition. As you would expect, her attitude is even more impressive than her surfing. In her interviews, she does not want to be identified as a disabled athlete, nor even distinguished as a female athlete, just an athlete like any other pro surfer.

COMMITMENT

Are you committed to excellence in the pursuit of your goals? Are you prepared to make the necessary sacrifices today to be the best you can be? It is important to draw a distinction here between commitment and working hard. To me, the former is shown by the person who is willing to make sacrifices, without a moment's hesitation, without thinking 'What am I giving up?' It's relocating for the right job, attending a weekend conference or work-related social occasion, it's dialling into an important meeting while on vacation.

The late Kobe Bryant, five-time NBA Champion and eighteen-time All-Star basketball player, once said, 'There's a choice that we have to make as people, as individuals. If you want to be great at something, there's a choice you have to make. We can all be masters at our craft, but you have to make a choice. What I mean by that is, there are inherent sacrifices that come along with that – family time, hanging out with friends, being a great friend, being a great son, nephew, whatever the case may be. There are sacrifices that come along with making that decision.' Bryant was not just talking about a physical commitment of effort, but what you have to give up in your life. While potentially tough for you, your family and friends at the time, such sacrifices will propel you further up the ladder, slowly but surely. Are you prepared to make them, as so many have done before you and as your competitors might be doing already?

Anyone not achieving their goals, not on the right path or hitting a plateau in their lives, can find at least one aspect of their plan, one area of their work where they can increase their commitment. This continued process of pushing harder and seeking out new opportunities is the driving force in getting us where we want to be.

COMMITMENT IS GIVING IT YOUR ALL

The level of commitment required to achieve your dreams is absolute. Anything less, and it's very unlikely that you'll attain your goals. In my early twenties, my career hit a serious plateau. Working in a low-level job at a performance tennis centre, I was feeling stuck. The only way to jump up a level was to commit more. To find the best players, fitness trainers and athletes in the world and learn from them.

FULL COMMITMENT IS LIFE-CHANGING

When I decided on a move to Australia, I wrote to every institute of sport, and state and national tennis centres there to set myself up with the opportunities I needed. I wrote to some many times until I got a response. I left my job, girlfriend, family and friends behind, with just a few hundred pounds and a credit card, and flew halfway across the globe to seek out the best. I fully committed and, once I had done that, I started to get luckier. Without this commitment, I wouldn't have progressed my career in the right direction for me.

EFFORT

Not achieving the goals you set for yourself? Have you plateaued? Ask yourself genuinely, how hard am I working? When you listen to and watch the very best in the world, one factor unites them – they will never be outworked by anyone. This in an incredibly simple concept, executed by very few. Most of us probably feel that we work hard, but in fact what we're usually doing is enough to get through the day-to-day. In order to get ahead, you have to put in more than everybody else. This is especially true when working on

The Extra Mile

Irish gymnast Kieran Behan has faced more adversity than most and always comes back with incredible effort and focus. Diagnosed with a tumour in his thigh at the age of eleven, he was wheelchair-bound for a year, suffering agonizing nerve damage during the operation to have it removed. Returning to the gym once back at full health, Behan had an accident in training, hitting his head on the horizontal bars, which resulted in a severe brain injury. He was told he'd never walk again. Refusing to accept his diagnosis, he picked himself up and retrained to reach international level once again. Yet, in another cruel twist of fate, in 2010 he ruptured both anterior cruciate ligaments on separate occasions. Against insurmountable odds he recovered, and at London 2012 he became only the second-ever gymnast to represent Ireland at an Olympic Games.

Finally, in the 2016 Rio Olympics, while competing fantastically well and looking to qualify for the finals, Behan dislocated his knee in the final exercise, leaving him in thirty-eighth place. After all of this, he was still undefeated: 'I know coming away from this, and in a few years' time or whatever, I know I'm going to be very, very proud of what I've done here … If I've inspired anyone out there, then that's what I'm going to be so proud of … You've got to find positivity and pick yourself back up and whatever happens, happens.'

a goal outside your normal day job. Pushing yourself above and beyond is the only way to exceed your current levels of performance and get the additional results you seek.

CONSISTENT HIGH EFFORT

The single hardest thing to do in your career comes when things are bad, you've had a major failure, a knock-back or a loss. I'm talking about showing up the next day with the right attitude and redoubling your efforts. Take note of these moments, even be excited by them. They will define your career and this is quite simply the only way to get through them.

EXTRA EFFORT

As famous entrepreneurs like Gary Vaynerchuk tell us, putting in a little extra effort every day can make a huge difference. You can get up earlier and do an hour of work towards that project which is going to propel you forward. You can dedicate your thoughts to it on your journey to work or spend the hour before you go to bed doing the same thing. When you would normally be sleeping or watching TV, this extra time adds up fast and you will thank yourself for investing it.

RELIABILITY

Are you someone who can simply get on with a job that you've got to do? Can you work under pressure, during stressful periods, time and time again? Would people describe you as dependable? Reliability is one of the chief qualities that employers look for. It's not easy to find people who turn up each day, on time, and do their job to the best of their ability. But reliability isn't just about turning up. If you can display this steadiness of hand, even during times of stress and pressure, that makes you an excellent team member.

Team Effort

When rowing as part of a team, even a minor relaxation from one member can drag down the whole boat's performance. So, to succeed at the top level regularly and reliably calls for an enormous commitment of time, effort, fitness and resolution throughout the year in all weathers. Dame Katherine Grainger, now Chair of UK Sport and Chancellor of Oxford Brookes University, is Britain's most decorated female Olympian. For three successive Olympics, from 2000 to 2008, Grainger won a silver medal – twice in the quadruple sculls, once in the coxless pairs.

At London 2012, the pressure she was under to perform in her own nation's Olympic Games must have been immense. Could she be relied upon again to be part of a medal-winning team? Would she finally go one further and secure the ultimate prize? In the semi-finals of the double sculls, Grainger broke the Olympic record to reach the final with her rowing partner, Anna Watkins. They went on to win gold in London. Grainger didn't stop there, training hard again to earn another silver in Rio 2016, before retiring from competitive sport with five Olympic medals, eight World Championship medals and seven Rowing World Cup wins under her belt.

A RELIABLE ASSET

There are very few people out there who can execute their jobs consistently with minimal fuss or drama. If you are someone who can, you possess a skill that may not feel that impressive, but which is more impactful than you think. Even greater still is an employee or team member who regularly goes above and beyond the call of duty and is proactive in solving issues.

UNSUNG RELIABILITY

I can think of many examples of sportspeople who are reliable. Who train and prepare properly, performing their jobs to the best of their ability, week in and week out. Often these individuals can be the unsung heroes of sports teams, who don't grab the headlines with a last-minute winning play, but are those who put in the work to create opportunities for others.

HUMILITY

Are you someone who prefers to impress people by telling them what you're going to achieve? Or, do you tend to under-promise and over-deliver? Can you genuinely say that you put others first, taking time, showing interest, demanding nothing from anyone that you wouldn't be prepared to do yourself? We all have egos. That internal desire for acknowledgement and respect. We all want to be appreciated for the job we've done. And that's fine, as long as we're grateful when it comes and don't feel entitled to it if it doesn't. It's important that we show humility when it comes to making mistakes, asking for help and ideas, as well as receiving feedback, both positive and negative, because this allows us to continually improve and learn.

HUMILITY SHOWS GRACE

In sport, low ego behaviour is scarce. But the best examples are when players show extraordinary levels of sportsmanship, putting their opponent's well-being ahead

The Humble Champion

Ask anyone who has followed tennis who the humblest tennis champion is, and Rafael Nadal will likely be the first name on their lips. You only need to listen to any of his pre- or post-match comments to get a very strong idea of the values with which he was raised. Firstly, there are never any excuses in defeat, always affording the maximum amount of credit to his opponent. No blame for conditions or circumstances, and pure accountability for what happened out on the court. Nadal's uncle, Toni, has coached him since he was three years old, instilling a discipline and humility in him as a player from the very beginning. 'I am happy when Rafa plays good tennis, but I take more pleasure when people say Rafael is a very good person. For me, it's so much more important to be a good person.' As Nadal once commented, 'Anyone can become a star, but everyone must be a human being.'

of their own glory. Like the Italian footballer Paolo Di Canio did in the dying minutes of one West Ham game, when the Everton goalkeeper Paul Gerrard was lying on the ground injured, leaving the goal wide open as the ball was crossed in. Di Canio caught the ball and halted the play. He felt he did exactly the right thing, as the keeper could have been seriously hurt, and in fact was later acknowledged with a FIFA Fair Play Award in 2001.

HUMILITY CAN DELIVER

The Tortoise is happy for others to think less of them and then pleasantly surprise people. The hidden genius in being humble is in making sure that you are over-prepared for any challenges that lie ahead. If, for example, regular public speaking is part of your job, it may be of some benefit to forget that you're good at it. Not so that nerves disable you on the day, but in order that you become incredibly thorough in your preparation, practising and leaving nothing to chance.

As we saw in Chapter One, a Tortoise is identifiable by basic characteristics such as loyalty, passion, positivity and generosity. All exist in every Tortoise to different degrees, no matter what type of Tortoise you are.

When we look at the values a Tortoise needs to win the race and become a successful Tortoise in life, however, we're going to a level beyond basic personality characteristics. Persistence, reliability, commitment and fortitude are just some of the values a successful Tortoise needs to develop. They can be worked on and improved over time. Unlike the Hare, the Tortoise always has time.

After reading this chapter, you're going to be taking the Tortoise Test to find out which values you need to focus on – a task that will point you directly to the relevant drills in Part Two, as you make your way towards Tortoise Boot Camp.

HOW DO YOU BECOME A WINNING TORTOISE?

- A Tortoise has certain basic characteristics, but a successful Tortoise needs to develop the clear values of patience, persistence, perspective, reliability, commitment, effort, humility and fortitude.

- Play the long game.

- Have faith in yourself and never quit.

- Overcome adversity and build success on it.

- Put in consistently high effort.

- Get on with the job and go the extra mile.

- Under-promise and over-deliver.

Take the
Tortoise Test

We've identified the characteristics and values that you need to develop to become a successful Tortoise. But as we've already touched upon, we each possess these traits to varying degrees. By finding out the areas in which you're lacking and doing the work to remedy it, you'll have the essential toolkit you need to reach whatever meaningful goals you set yourself.

I've designed this test to help you to assess your current standings in relation to both your basic characteristics as a Tortoise and the values that make Tortoises successful. Through it, you'll be able to acknowledge your own strengths and prioritize areas of weakness. Thinking about this may also help you to decide which type of Tortoise development profile you fit.

Depending on how much of a Tortoise you turn out to be, there are four stages of development: Twilight; Tyro; Typical; and True:

Twilight – a hybrid between Tortoise and Hare; which way do you want to go?

Tyro – a Tortoise in training; are you prepared to do the work to become Typical?

Typical – you're clearly committed; do you want to upgrade to True?

True – the complete Tortoise, but how can you become even better?

As with any test, you'll need to be really honest in your answers to get the most out of it. The whole point of it is to identify areas for improvement, so please don't go for the answer you feel is best, but rather the one that best reflects you. We are going to address the characteristics and values we've been discussing and you'll rate yourself with a score of one to three, depending on how well you are demonstrating each value in your life right now.

3	Constantly display this behaviour, no matter what the circumstances.
2	Occasionally display this behaviour, but not always.
1	Rarely/never display this behaviour.

1   I stand up for work colleagues if they aren't in the room and someone else is saying negative things about them.
Score 1 / 2 / 3

2   I speak with conviction about subjects I really care about in all situations, be it meetings, casual conversations at lunch or phone calls to my friends.
Score 1 / 2 / 3

3   When I'm in a tough position and those around me are being negative, I see the positives in the situation and put them forward.
Score 1 / 2 / 3

4   I recognize that generosity of spirit towards others is not only the best way to get a positive outcome in a situation, but also feels better.
Score 1 / 2 / 3

5   I can wait for the success I want, even though it's going to take a long time to reach.
Score 1 / 2 / 3

6   When things are becoming frustrating and I'm feeling pressure to quit, I stick with a task.
Score 1 / 2 / 3

7   I play the long game because I have faith in myself to succeed.
Score 1 / 2 / 3

8 Even in the darkest of days, I retain the courage of my convictions and remain purposeful.
Score 1 / 2 / 3

9 I commit to excellence and understand that achieving it demands making tough sacrifices.
Score 1 / 2 / 3

10 I work hard and am prepared to put in consistently high effort day to day.
Score 1 / 2 / 3

11 When given a job to do, I simply get on with it and keep going until the task is complete.
Score 1 / 2 / 3

12 When I've done a good job, I prefer to pleasantly surprise people rather than tell them about it.
Score 1 / 2 / 3

13 I can be trusted to achieve any task that I'm set to very high standards.
Score 1 / 2 / 3

14 I'm happy to take my time winning people over and don't mind if my good work goes unnoticed and underappreciated in the beginning.
Score 1 / 2 / 3

15 I may move slowly, but I'm 100 per cent determined to succeed.
Score 1 / 2 / 3

WHAT'S THE SCORE?

Once you've given yourself a score for each and totalled them up, take a look at the table below and see where you're at.

41–45 **TRUE**	Total Tortoise! You'll get there in your own time and you'll win. Only two or three areas to strengthen.
36–40 **TYPICAL**	Tortoise with commitment. You may still have up to nine areas you can work on.
31–35 **TYRO**	Tortoise in training. Lots of Tortoise-like characteristics, some weaknesses. You'll need to strengthen almost every characteristic and value.
26–30 **TWILIGHT**	Tortoise or Hare? You share characteristics of both, so could improve either way. If you decide to follow the way of the Tortoise, first you must commit.
25 and **below**	Admit it, you're a Hare who just likes doing tests!

The overall score will place you at a Tortoise development level that points to just how much work you're going to need to do to become a truly successful Tortoise. For example, even a Typical Tortoise who scores 3 for six of the statements will still have work to do on the remaining nine areas. While a Tyro Tortoise could excel at eight of the statements and have a huge amount to improve upon on the remaining seven. Even a Twilight Tortoise, currently a hybrid, could excel in seven Tortoise values and find itself with hard graft required for the other eight.

The next step is to look at your individual scores and pick out the responses where you scored 1 or 2. Then use the directions below to understand how you need to improve in that area and which drill(s) to follow in Part Two.

Statement 1: I stand up for work colleagues if they aren't in the room and someone else is saying negative things about them.

If you scored 1 or 2, then you're low to medium on loyalty. Do some work on communication, assertiveness and team building.

Try the following drills in Part Two:

Communicate the Tortoise way
Develop a Tortoise team culture
Manage conflict
Take your job seriously, but not yourself

Statement 2: I speak with conviction about subjects I really care about in all situations, be it meetings, casual conversations at lunch or phone calls to my friends.

Low scores here show you're lacking in passion at work. Identify what you really care about, find your passion and talk to people.

Try the following drills in Part Two:

Deal with success
Take care of yourself, family and loved ones

Statement 3: When I'm in a tough position and those around me are being negative, I see the positives in the situation and put them forward.

If you can't see the positives, are you allowing your working life to get on top of you? If you can see them but aren't speaking up, what's holding you back?

Try the following drills in Part Two:

Communicate the Tortoise way
Deal with pressure
Deal with failure
Manage conflict

Statement 4: I recognize that generosity of spirit towards others is not only the best way to get a positive outcome in a situation, but also feels better.

Are you struggling to get what you want in challenging situations? Break this vicious circle by getting to know and understand your teammates better.

Try the following drills in Part Two:

> Communicate the Tortoise way
> Develop a Tortoise team culture
> Play two or three moves ahead

Statement 5: I can wait for the success I want, even though it's going to take a long time to reach.

This is one of the more difficult areas, which most people have to work at. Unscrupulous Hares can take advantage of the fact that patience (in others) is seen as a virtue.

Try the following drills in Part Two:

> Develop a Tortoise team culture
> Deal with success
> Play two or three moves ahead
> Take your job seriously, but not yourself

Statement 6: When things are becoming frustrating and I'm feeling pressure to quit, I stick with a task.

'Nobody likes a quitter' is a horrible phrase, but one we can learn from. There may be many workplace and personal reasons why you're struggling to stick at something.

Try the following drills in Part Two:

> Deal with pressure
> Deal with failure
> Manage conflict
> Take your job seriously, but not yourself
> Take care of yourself, family and loved ones

Statement 7: I play the long game because I have faith in myself to succeed.

If you're struggling with confidence and lacking faith in yourself, you'll likely be feeling alone and unsupported. Only you can break this cycle. As hard as it may seem, try to focus on communicating with your colleagues to make meaningful connections.

Try the following drills in Part Two:

> Communicate the Tortoise way
> Play two or three moves ahead
> Manage change
> Lead by taking action

Statement 8: Even in the darkest of days, I retain the courage of my convictions and remain purposeful.

It's extremely honest to admit to struggling with adversity, even to yourself. Nobody wants to advertise a lack of resilience. Low scores here may mean that in order to pick up the fortitude you need, you could try looking at your life beyond work and focus on what you really care about.

Try the following drills in Part Two:

> Take your job seriously, but not yourself
> Take care of yourself, family and loved ones

Statement 9: I commit to excellence and understand that achieving it demands making tough sacrifices.

We all want to score highly with this one. If we're true to ourselves, we may have to admit to wanting our cake and eating it. We desire the top jobs with the top people. But what does it take? Don't beat yourself up about it. Open up to your colleagues and find out where they are with commitment and focus.

Try the following drills in Part Two:

> Communicate the Tortoise way
> Develop a Tortoise team culture
> Deal with pressure
> Manage change
> Work well with successful high achievers

Statement 10: I work hard and am prepared to put in consistently high effort day to day.

If you've been brave enough to face up to not achieving this statement, well done. You'll be making lots of effort when you reach Tortoise Boot Camp at the end of this book. For now, listening to your teammates and being prepared for the changes to come will be your work in progress.

Try the following drills in Part Two:

> Develop a Tortoise team culture
> Manage change

Statement 11: When given a job to do, I simply get on with it and keep going until the task is complete.

There are many reasons why it could be difficult for anybody to get on with a job, from absence of direction to a lack of resources. But let's assume that everything is in place, so there's something here that's troubling you. Could it be boredom? If you want to be more reliable, it's time to remind yourself about your end goal.

Try the following drills in Part Two:

> Lead by taking action
> Take care of yourself, family and loved ones

Statement 12: When I've done a good job, I prefer to pleasantly surprise people rather than tell them about it.

If you second-guessed this one, knowing how Hares like to tell everyone all around them how good they are, you'll have given yourself a 3. But you're reading this, so you know you occasionally need acknowledgement for good work like anyone else. To help you to hold yourself back at such times and let your work do the talking for you, put some time into developing good listening skills.

Try the following drills in Part Two:

> Communicate the Tortoise way
> Develop a Tortoise team culture

Statement 13: I can be trusted to achieve any task that I'm set to very high standards.

Trustworthiness is one of the key values that we look for in people we work with, but we are only human and it is difficult to give 100 per cent all the time. If you scored below a 3 here, you've just signed up for doing some work on your energy levels and consistency.

Try the following drills in Part Two:

> Develop a Tortoise team culture
> Take your job seriously, but not yourself
> Work well with successful high achievers
> Take care of yourself, family and loved ones

Statement 14: I'm happy to take my time winning people over and don't mind if my good work goes unnoticed and underappreciated in the beginning.

A low score here could reveal an issue with impatience. On the other hand, it might point to a highly competitive culture in which people only get ahead by being noticed. If you're interested in developing further as a Tortoise, you'll find the time to step back from worrying about your profile and let the Hares get ahead. Your time will come.

Try the following drills in Part Two:

> Develop a Tortoise team culture
> Play two or three moves ahead
> Take your job seriously, but not yourself
> Lead by taking action

Statement 15: I may move slowly, but I'm 100 per cent determined to succeed.

It seems obvious to say it, but no Tortoise moves quickly. It's the nature of the beast. If you've recognized yourself as a Tortoise, perhaps your focus in this statement is more on that 100 per cent determination to succeed than the pace. As your score could be better, it's worthwhile putting in some work on developing resilience and staying power.

Try the following drills in Part Two:

> Deal with pressure
> Deal with failure
> Deal with success

REGULARLY RESET YOUR TORTOISE MINDSET

Having done this test for the first time, make sure that you keep your scores and repeat this exercise in four to six weeks' time. This is a great tool for grounding yourself, bringing you back to what is ultimately important to you and helping you to recognize the qualities that will allow you to achieve your goals. The other reason for doing this is that these Tortoise characteristics and values can often be in a state of flux. Depending on what is happening to you at any given time, you may find your weakest values slipping a little. Regular re-evaluation will ensure that they don't slip too far.

Like any data- or information-gathering, context is imperative when looking back and reviewing how your scores have changed. Therefore, one final piece of the puzzle here is to make a few small notes, like a diary, at the bottom of each re-test to describe your activity for that month. Was it a high-pressure/high-stress period of work? Conversely, was it a very successful/happy spell? How did this affect your scores? Reflecting on how your behaviour changes under differing circumstances can help you to take a large step towards becoming a successful Tortoise and prepare you for situations that you know will arise in the future.

For example, if you know you have a lot to achieve in your final sales quarter of the year and are aware that you often lack positivity and urgency when under pressure, choosing to be negative about others and procrastinating, you can get ready for this in advance and be vigilant around these behaviours for the next quarter. This practice can help your performance and pleasantly surprise your colleagues, who may have already noticed these negative behaviour patterns in you in the past.

If you repeat this process often enough, you will start to develop a level of self-awareness, whereby you can self-regulate in the moment. As situations arise which test these Tortoise values, you will consciously choose the right action for you as a Tortoise. Take loyalty as an example. You may find yourself in a situation where colleagues are criticizing another person behind their back. Having regularly done your Tortoise Test, you will be aware that this is an area which is important to improve upon or maintain a higher score on by removing yourself from those conversations. Or, better still, by gently challenging what is being said and sticking up for your teammate.

Part Two

TORTOISE GOES TO BOOT CAMP

4

A SUCCESSFUL TORTOISE
NEEDS SOFT SKILLS

Welcome to Part Two. Having built on our understanding of why the way of the Tortoise is the only truly sustainable path to success, and what it really means to be a Tortoise, it's now time to turn our attention from getting into the right mindset to forming, using and then sharpening those skills that will transform you into the powerful, successful Tortoise you've always wanted to be.

In this part of the book we will focus on taking guided, practical action to develop the values you identified as lacking when you took the Tortoise Test. Whether you rated yourself as a Twilight Tortoise or a True Tortoise or somewhere in between, you can still make the improvements you need by putting in the effort to hone your abilities.

Before we get to it, let me outline for you what's coming up as you progress through the second part of the book. In the next chapter, you'll get into the drills that will help you to shape up as a more effective Tortoise, from communicating the Tortoise way, dealing with pressure and playing two or three moves ahead to understanding the behaviour of the highly successful. While you can try them all, it's best to initially target those that correspond to your areas of need. In Chapter Six, we'll explore how a Tortoise can operate successfully at different career stages, from pre-entry wannabe all the way to an upper-management influencer twenty years down the line. In Chapter Seven, we'll explore the major challenges facing aspirational people like you: how to get your ideas and concepts across to people who have the authority or financial power to implement them. Here, I'll introduce you to my Tortoise buy-in matrix – a useful tool for thinking about how to influence people at various stages with your ideas, assessing the likelihood of success and required effort.

Ultimately, when you think you're ready to try out your knowledge and skills, I'm going to put you through a week-long, day-by-day Tortoise Boot Camp. Not just to test your skills for three different entry-level stages, but also to provide you with exercises in three different categories:

→ Skills for existing situations you can action immediately

→ Skills for upcoming situations you can plan for

→ Skills for longer-term situations you're likely to meet

To survive Tortoise Boot Camp, you'll have to commit the time, make sacrifices and put in the effort as we look at the importance of soft skills in addition to maximizing those essential Tortoise characteristics and approaches.

SOFT SKILLS

So, what exactly are soft skills and why are they so important? Over 100 years ago, the shock of the First World War combined with the emergence of the field of psychology to produce an important study about successful leaders. A team from Harvard University, the Carnegie Foundation and Stanford Research Centre published the results of the study in 1918, which found that 85 per cent of job success comes from having well-developed people skills.

When American physicist, educator and war adviser to the US government, Charles Riborg Mann, who led the research, asked 30,000 engineering society members to number the top six qualities required for success, they were clear: character, judgement, efficiency, understanding of men (all engineers were men at the time), knowledge and technique. And here we had the first description of what we today call 'soft skills'.

In 2004, Harvard was still researching this subject of leadership in business, asking hundreds of multinational companies, 'What makes a leader?' What had changed? Psychologist and author of this report, Daniel Goleman, found that the one quality which made the best leaders in these organizations stand out from the rest was having a high degree of emotional intelligence. The concept of emotional intelligence first appeared in the 1960s, when psychologists began distinguishing between this and traditional types of intelligence, as classified by IQ. By the 1980s, psychologist Howard Gardner was talking about 'multiple intelligences', differentiating between those of an 'interpersonal' and 'intrapersonal' nature. So, emotional intelligence had now acquired its own field of study, combining on one hand the capacity to understand the intentions, motivations and desires of other people and, on the other, the ability to understand oneself, to appreciate one's feelings, fears and motivations. In the mid-1990s, Goleman himself wrote a bestseller called *Emotional Intelligence*. The earlier phrase had stuck.

It seems clear, therefore, that a combination of people, social and communication skills could be the magic recipe for leadership success, rather than purely acquired skills, or Hare values such as innate superiority, natural talent and charismatic personality. These latter Hare values still seem to trump the findings we've known about for so many generations. Perhaps many still regard emotional intelligence and soft skills as flaky and dispensable. Or perhaps jumping the queue and perpetuating inequality of opportunity are just more effective Hare tactics.

Assuming that hard-skill levels are equal among the leaders he surveyed for his 2004 report, Goleman established that having higher levels of emotional intelligence formed 90 per cent of the factors that would propel some further up the corporate ladder than their counterparts. The truth is that we know what makes successful leaders, but still seem reluctant to provide training in it. Is that because we don't like the 'soft' sound of soft skills? It's probably because, unlike many hard skills, it's difficult to measure common sense and a positive attitude.

In his study, Goleman highlights four foundational stages of emotional intelligence: self-awareness, self-regulation, empathy and skilful relationships. The Hare rarely bothers with these. But, to become a successful Tortoise, they are where your work lies. All twelve drills in the next chapter will help you to develop your soft skills:

1 Communicate the Tortoise way

2 Develop a Tortoise team culture

3 Deal with pressure

4 Deal with failure

5 Deal with success

6 Play two or three moves ahead

7 Manage change

8 Manage conflict

9 Take your job seriously, but not yourself

10 Work well with successful high achievers

11 Lead by taking action

12 Take care of yourself, family and loved ones

Hard skills are a given for a successful career. You won't get far without them. But you can learn them academically and on the job. Soft skills are essential. You won't get very far with your hard skills if you don't have the soft skills that communicate how you see yourself and the people around you in your chosen profession. They're more difficult to learn and acquire, but when you do it will place you ahead of your competitors.

A TORTOISE NEEDS A HARD SHELL

Here are a couple of questions for you to ponder. Is a Tortoise slow because it carries a hard, heavy shell? Or, does a Tortoise need to carry a hard, heavy shell because it is slow by nature? Before we move on to drills and exercises, we need to explore our natural human responses to stress or trauma.

Many of you will have heard of the original theory of 'fight or flight' responses that were set out over a century ago by Walter Bradford Cannon, an American physiologist at Harvard Medical School. He determined that, when presented by a threat, animals and humans alike will either stand and fight back or run away to avoid the danger. This is an automatic response by the sympathetic nervous system to physiologically prepare the body for one of those options. More recently, when looking at human behaviour, other conscious choices have been added to the list of two, which include:

> **Freeze:** whereby the response is to be frozen to the spot, much like a deer caught in the headlights of a car;

> **Flooding:** where a person is completely overcome with emotion;

> **Fawn:** becoming submissive, even to the point of attempting to befriend the aggressor;

> **Fatigue:** to sleep or take regular naps in response to high stress, more prominent in children.

Though far from being a behavioural psychologist, I would like to add in one of my own here. This is simply something

I have observed a great deal in life, as well as being a tactic I've often employed:

> **Framing:** do not react, simply watch and wait to see how the situation unfolds, calmly and with composure.

When faced with a stressful set of circumstances, people react according to their personality type, past experience and their emotional status on that given day. The trick is to train yourself not to react, to do nothing at first, and just observe and patiently monitor how things develop. This does not have to mean being passive, or freezing, or being submissive and allowing things to simply happen to us. It means having poise, the confidence not to react. You take emotional ownership of the situation through the power of simply holding your position.

Later in the book, I'll go on to talk about the importance of just showing up, being there for others. Saying nothing and just having a presence can help someone who is in a state of stress. The act of maintaining your position is very similar to this. It's useful when experiencing conflict, change or debate in the workplace, or even just being in an awkward or uncomfortable situation, like not knowing anyone at a party. It also allows issues or people to come to you, rather than you seeking them out. This puts you in a powerful place. In my view, waiting to see how others react, before selecting your own response, is the best stance to take. But it does require a certain amount of self-assuredness. Like any skill, though, practice breeds self-confidence as you improve at it. A Tortoise needs to hold its position and for that it requires a hard shell. And soft skills within that hard shell.

DEVELOPING 'FEEL'

Some people prefer the word empathy, but for me, feel works much better and I often use the word in my own work. Developing feel is such an important skill not only in your job but also in life. Being aware of a situation, putting yourself in the shoes of every single person there, making sure you form a connection with the person or group on what they truly want, asking the right question to elicit this response, genuinely listening to their answer and asking further questions. It's about being clear about what they want, how they feel, how they think you can help them.

All too often, we have already decided for someone else what we think they want. Ever done that? Whether right or wrong, you did not create or maintain a bond by asking and listening first. If you want to develop a bond of trust, you need first to listen, then follow this up with a statement that lets a person know you've heard them. This validates their emotion, the way they are feeling about an experience. Whether this is a positive experience – 'I'm so excited for you', 'I'm glad that this is happening for you', 'You deserve this' – or a negative one – 'I'm so sorry this has happened to you', 'I can see how difficult this must be for you'. Only when you have truly listened and validated what someone has said should you move on to what they would like you to do to help them.

It is really important that you train yourself to get better at developing empathy, just like any other skill. The good news is, opportunities for doing this in your working and personal life may present themselves every day. Pick out an upcoming meeting, a decision, a competition or any pivotal moment. This could be for your team or an individual whom you work with, or even a family member. There are two ways to develop this skill. The first is to prepare for the mood or feelings of each colleague in your chosen situation, *in advance*:

> Ask yourself how each person will hope this turns out. How do you think it will affect that individual? What will they be worried about?

Make notes based on the conversations you've had with all the individuals involved and pick out key statements, feelings and projections that your colleagues have made. If people are stressed, it's important to note that they may have catastrophized the situation in their mind or even over-exaggerated the positives. Note where these views may differ within a group and take account of potential clashes of agenda. Having a grasp for this in advance will help you in your approach to that situation and align your communication to the best outcome.

The second method is to be very *reflective* of your own behaviour. That doesn't mean sitting for an hour each night analysing yourself. After your chosen meeting/decision/competition/pivotal moment, simply make some notes below your preparatory ones, asking:

> Did I say the right thing? What would the people I interacted with think of what I said and how I said it? Who might I have upset, made happy, impressed with what I said? How could I have been better?

Then, compare the two sets of notes to see how well you achieved the outcomes set out beforehand.

A final point of reflection ought to be asking yourself:

> Did I listen actively and show that I was listening?
> How much did I know about each person's concerns
> or hopes for the outcome? Did I hear something
> new that arose out of the situation? Why wasn't I
> aware of this before? Did anyone express opinions I
> couldn't grasp? Whose views surprised me?

The more experience you gain in preparing for and reflecting on situations that occur, the more accurate your instincts will be. Your intuition will become far more attuned to the needs of others and make listening to your gut far more reliable. This can also help you to be mindful as you do this live, at the moment of interaction, allowing you to make adjustments in your approach and style of communication.

Making mistakes in developing feel is actually one of the most important aspects of a young professional's development. You may offer your opinion too readily to those with more experience, say too much in a meeting, suggest bad advice or simply not listen properly. Today, whenever I see this happening, I know how vital it is to point out such behaviour in a firm but kind way. Doing this at an early stage can save someone from becoming a Hare later in their career.

YOU AND YOUR SOFT SKILLS

- When we talk about soft skills, we are referring to people skills, social skills, communication skills.

- You'll need to work at your emotional intelligence: self-awareness, self-regulation, empathy and skilful relationships.

- You're a Tortoise, you're slower than the Hare, so you must recognize the worth of a hard exterior and learn how to hold your position.

- Considering the needs and feelings of others is not only the best way to climb the career ladder – it's also the most effective way to be in life!

5

TWELVE DRILLS FOR SOFT SKILLS

Let's turn our attention now to the drills and exercises that will help you to improve your score on the Tortoise Test by developing and enhancing those all-important soft skills that a successful Tortoise needs. By working your way through these, you'll be adopting methods that enable you to work well with colleagues and be looked upon favourably by management. As a Tortoise, you'll be practising techniques that play to your strengths and hone the values you've come to recognize as your own.

As I mentioned at the end of the last chapter, I want to be very situation-specific regarding soft skills. Subjects like creative thinking and time management are all well and good, but they don't arm you for your first encounter with a high-achieving individual or dealing with failure. These are very real and commonly occurring situations which many people get wrong, no matter what their experience. So, whether you're a middle manager or an entry-level Tortoise, the drills here are likely to be just as relevant, useful and effective.

1 Communicate the Tortoise way
2 Develop a Tortoise team culture
3 Deal with pressure

4 Deal with failure

5 Deal with success

6 Play two or three moves ahead

7 Manage change

8 Manage conflict

9 Take your job seriously, but not yourself

10 Work well with successful high achievers

11 Lead by taking action

12 Take care of yourself, family and loved ones

1 COMMUNICATE THE TORTOISE WAY

Use this drill to improve your Tortoise Test score on the following statements:

- I stand up for work colleagues if they aren't in the room and someone else is saying negative things about them.

- When I'm in a tough position in life, I see the positives in the situation and put them forward.

- I recognize that generosity of spirit towards others is not only the best way to get a positive outcome in a situation, but also feels better.

- I play the long game because I have faith in myself to succeed.

- I commit to excellence and understand that achieving it demands making tough sacrifices.

- When I've done a good job, I prefer to pleasantly surprise people rather than tell them about it.

From minutiae to global issues, so many problems are caused by a lack of understanding or a failure of communication. Down the years, I've often bemoaned going to meetings which I felt didn't relate to me directly, spending hours talking about subjects that didn't particularly interest me. But this was the wrong attitude. Even if the meeting didn't tackle the exact issues I wanted to discuss, I was still in a room with my colleagues, listening to concerns affecting the department, company or industry I was working in. Messages would have been sinking in about opportunities that could be taken advantage of and how my co-workers were reacting to developments. Chances to be involved in group conversation with one's peers should be seen as a positive opportunity to develop. Here are some steps I have taken to make sure my communication is at the right level.

STEP 1: OVER-COMMUNICATE

While the quality of communication is an important factor, almost all problems can be solved with more communication, not less. By this I don't mean 1,000-word emails on every subject. Instead, regular conversations, whether face to face or even instant messenger group chats, will suffice.

STEP 2: BE ACCOUNTABLE FOR ALL COMMUNICATION

Avoid blaming others for a lack of communication. So often in life I hear, 'No one has told me what's going on' or 'The communication has been poor'. And I always wonder, 'Why didn't you make it your business to find out what's going on?' It's important to take accountability for not being informed. If I really want to speak to someone, to find out some information or even to pass some on, I will make it my business to do so. I'll call, follow up with a text, call again and leave a message and repeat this process until I hear back from them. If others have missed vital information that you could've shared, take some ownership of this too, even if it's starting an instant messenger chat or email thread to include those people in the future.

STEP 3: LISTEN

Listening is the central aspect of good communication. Taking the time to properly hear what a person is saying is very different to just allowing the other person to talk while you think of your next brilliant point. If you respond to someone by making your own statement which does not relate to their subject, they will assume you haven't been listening and they're probably right. Instead, validate their emotion or statement with an affirmation: 'I understand', 'That must be tough for you' or 'That's great, I'm so excited for you'. Then offer your view on that specific subject, before adjusting to your own agenda, if you have one. To reaffirm that you're a good listener, make sure that the next time you communicate with that person, ask them questions about the subject they were talking about the last time you spoke.

STEP 4: BE SIMPLE, BE CONCISE, BE CLEAR

When communicating with others, make yourself almost painfully clear, especially when giving instructions. Of course, don't speak to colleagues as if they were five-year-olds; just ensure that they leave knowing precisely your point of view or exactly what you want them to do. Break

Negotiating Life or Death

With so much at stake in high-pressure hostage situations, communication is key and faultless interaction with the perpetrator can mean the difference between life and death. Sergeant Scott Tillema is an FBI-trained hostage negotiator who spent over seven years as part of a SWAT team undertaking this type of work and has spoken eloquently about the skills required when he was called to a house over a potential suicide threat. When he entered the property and made his way down to the basement, he found a man sitting in an armchair, holding a gun to his head. Tillema immediately introduced himself and offered to help him, quickly establishing rapport. He noticed the guy was now staring at him instead of at the floor. Things were starting to look more positive. Then, the suicidal man asked if they were going to take him to the hospital. In his rush to help, Sergeant Tillema instantly said, 'Yes, of course we will take you to the hospital.' At this point, the atmosphere changed for the worse. By his own admission, Tillema had failed to establish an understanding of what this man actually wanted and the trust was broken. The last place in the world the man had actually wanted to go was to the hospital. His team negotiated with the man for eighteen hours, but he still shot himself (though he survived the gunshot wound). It was a harsh lesson for Tillema.

it down into very simple terminology and repeat it. Be concise in your message. Don't use twenty words where one will do. Avoid using overly technical language to sound sophisticated. If they get it wrong, don't blame them; blame yourself for not making it clear enough.

Try this communication exercise:
Seek out a person with whom you don't communicate particularly well. This could be for any reason – a language barrier, shyness, friction between you or simply a clash of personalities. Then, try this exercise over a couple of weeks.

Stage 1: Start a conversation with them and form a connection around a mutually interesting project/ upcoming event/meeting/decision. Prepare for it with the 'developing feel' exercise at the end of the last chapter.

Stage 2: Employ the four rules of communication over a two-week period – over-communicate; take responsibility for all communication; listen; be clear and simple.

Stage 3: After a week, review how well your interaction has gone with that individual, based on the four rules. Ask yourself some of the empathy review questions. Did I say the right thing? What would the people with whom I interacted think of what I said and how I said it? Who might I have upset, made happy, impressed with what I said? How could I have communicated more successfully?

Stage 4: Set out your plan for the following week. Look at improving from your feedback in Stage 3. Which of the four communication rules could you implement better?

Stage 5: At the end of the fortnight, think about the connection you now have with that individual in the following way:

Yes or No?

- Are you more at ease in their company?

- Has conversation become free-flowing?

- Do you share similar opinions on your chosen situation?

- Were you able to disagree without discomfort/ awkwardness?

- How often do they initiate communication with you now, compared to before?

- Are you having more face-to-face interactions now?

- Has body language since changed (eye contact, facing each other, arms unfolded, etc.) in your communications?

Yes? If the answer to one or more of these questions is yes, be pleased with your progress and congratulate yourself for going out of your comfort zone to make this happen. Whether you've made a friend out of that colleague or not, improving the communication with anyone in your immediate environment can only be a positive thing.

No? Even if the answer is no to all of the questions, do not be disheartened. There could be a plethora of reasons for someone else's level of communication which has nothing to do with you, your personality or actions. Of every five people you meet, one may simply not like you. This is just an unavoidable likelihood. It certainly shouldn't shut the door to you being the persistent Tortoise and trying to reach out to that same person at a later date. The result in the future could be a very different one!

Communication Tip
Making an assumption about what someone else wants rarely works out. Listen to the person first.

2 DEVELOP A TORTOISE TEAM CULTURE

Use this drill to improve your Tortoise Test score on the following statements:

- I stand up for work colleagues if they aren't in the room and someone else is saying negative things about them.

- I recognize that generosity of spirit towards others is not only the best way to get a positive outcome in a situation, but also feels better.

- I can wait for the success I want, even though it's going to take a long time to reach.

- I commit to excellence and understand that achieving it demands making tough sacrifices.

- I work hard and am prepared to put in consistently high effort day to day.

- When I've done a good job, I prefer to pleasantly surprise people rather than tell them about it.

- I can be trusted to achieve any task that I'm set to very high standards.

- I'm happy to take my time winning people over and don't mind if my good work goes unnoticed and underappreciated in the beginning.

Building and maintaining a strong cohesion within a team of people in order to implement a commonly held goal is truly one of the most difficult tasks in the workplace. Ask any manager about the most challenging aspect of their role, and managing staff will be very close to the top of the list. Even in small teams, the mix of different personalities, backgrounds and value sets can be vast.

Pulling this all together takes strong leadership, but that's not what I want to emphasize in this drill. Instead, I want to focus on questions around the soft skills of the individuals in that group, which enable a strong team culture to establish and flourish:

> 'How can you be the best teammate you can be?'
> 'How can you contribute in a way that makes life
> better for the team and your manager? 'What
> behaviours can you display, without being led, that
> will aid the task, even if you are not acknowledged
> for it?'

This is very much the Tortoise mindset at work. As opposed to that of the Hare, which would be more akin to 'How can I dictate this situation to either work out the best for me and empower me over others, or so that I can succeed in the task and gain acknowledgement?'

This is why I want to spend a bit more time here to give you an appreciation of the different dynamics that are always at play within any team structure. There is definitely a need to have a balance of both Hare and Tortoise influence within a team. Depending on the balance of power between those individuals, it will have an impact on the cohesiveness of the unit and, most likely, the success in achieving the task.

If you're a Tortoise in the team environment, where do you position yourself in the team dynamic? Do you simply remain quiet and passive to the demands of the Hares around you? Of course not. Tortoises must be patient and accepting of the Hares they work with. As they are often the creators providing the drive, you mustn't stifle them, but rather allow them to thrive. Therefore, consciously allowing them the space and freedom to work is not sacrificing control or influence, but simply good teamwork.

Tortoise decision-making is more often based on experience than the instinctual nature of a Hare. While this approach is the preferable one in many situations, if there's time pressure or a lack of information upon which to base a decision, the Hare ought to be given the scope to be a major influence on the process.

If a Tortoise is being managed by a Hare, it is important to recognize the difference between a passive approach and a submissive one. The Tortoise can manage the Hare 'from below', by using their experience and more rational nature as a steadying influence on decision-making. As always, choosing the right time and place to deliver such messages is important, but this is also second nature to the Tortoise.

Allowing Hares to run riot with a free rein over a team is seldom a good situation, which is why it's important to have a balance of both 'species' in an organization. By the same token, allowing a group of Tortoises to work together will likely produce less creative and dynamic results.

Now we have gained an appreciation of differing team dynamics, and embraced the theory of developing a Tortoise team culture, let's look at steps for how you can become a great Tortoise team player immediately.

Take responsibility for implementing these steps yourself. Do not wait for others to lead the way and then just follow in their footsteps. Even if you haven't been appointed a leader, be a shining example to inspire others. Essentially, you are simply exhibiting behaviours that any manager wants to see and every other team member wants to be involved with. There are only positives for you in adopting these behaviours.

STEP 1: ACCEPT DIFFERENCE

Members of any team must accept each other's idiosyncrasies. We all have quirks, habits and even tastes that vary. With the wrong mindset, these can create friction. You don't have to celebrate each other's differences, but simply be patient with them. Accept that, as dissimilar as someone else is to you, you are also to them.

STEP 2: LISTEN TO EACH OTHER

You must counsel each other. What gets you through tough times isn't necessarily the large formal team meeting about all the issues, it's the ten-minute chat with teammates on the way to the train station, the lunch, the pub, the two-minute walk to the meeting. You'll find that listening, allowing your colleagues to vent their fears, frustrations, ideas, dreams, then getting the same respect back, genuinely nips things in the bud. You actually self-manage as a team.

STEP 3: MAKE IT HONEST

One of the mottos of the strongest team I worked with was 'Internally honest, externally strong'. Of course, behind closed doors there has to be honesty. In fact, the most uncomfortable exercise I've ever done was to go around the table, face to face with this team, telling everyone the things they could improve upon, or what they were doing that didn't work. The 'externally strong' aspect is something that I truly admire in good teams and is immediately apparent about them. They work for each other, they 'have each other's backs' and would never allow outside criticism to influence them. Manchester United's legendary manager, Sir Alex Ferguson, would always defend his team when speaking to the press, yet you could always imagine that, once back in the locker room, he would let the players know in no uncertain terms how he felt about a performance.

STEP 4: USE HUMOUR

A trick I've learned in the last few years is that using humour can be a great feedback tool, especially for difficult subjects. It simply beats berating that person in the first instance. Take, for example, tardiness. The first time someone is late for a meeting, a few comments like 'Oh, here he is!' or 'Finally thought you'd join us, eh?' from the right person in the team can be a softer way of dealing with an issue. Of course, for repeat offenders something sterner is required.

STEP 5: HEAR THE MESSAGE

The ability to listen to your teammates – what an underappreciated skill this is! But you have to listen so that you can hear. Allowing people to finish what they are saying before you speak is such a simple but vital act towards good

Hares Within Team Environments

In 2002, fiery Manchester United captain Roy Keane walked out of the Ireland national football team's training camp during preparations for a World Cup quarter final. Against all the odds, Keane had led the Irish side to qualify for the 2002 World Cup hosted by Japan and South Korea. It had been a long time since Ireland had reached the final stages of this prestigious event and, with their talismanic captain leading the way, the nation was full of excitement. However, issues around the standards of the training facilities and the equipment that had been provided for Ireland's use began to arise and Keane's patience with manager Mick McCarthy was wearing thin.

In the view of the former, the team should have had the same level of facilities that he was used to using at Manchester United (a powerhouse of domestic and European football). Keane allegedly abused McCarthy in front of the players and the international press, and then flew home (whether this was by choice or not remains unknown). The Irishman now looks back on this incident with regret, because representing your country in a World Cup competition is one of the highest honours a footballer can achieve. If you look at how well Keane was managed at Manchester United by Sir Alex Ferguson, who adopted a famously autocratic leadership style by giving players the 'hairdryer treatment' (shouting at them), such issues never arose. Keane clearly respected Ferguson and they were very successful in working together. That was until towards the end of Keane's playing career, when Ferguson felt that it was time for him to leave Manchester United, and they fell out publicly and irreversibly. Once the respect had been lost, the two Hares clashed, and this never ends well.

communication. And you're far more likely to hear what they say and get the message.

STEP 6: GIVE PRAISE

Working in an environment of positivity and support is well proven to be more productive. Happy people get more done, in general. One of the tricks I've used is to pay teammates unexpected compliments. It's even more effective if you call them over for a word with a stern look on your face. Then, when they get to you, tell them how awesome they are because of a small thing that you noticed they did, but that no one else would probably have seen. Believe me, this is a really powerful tool to motivate a colleague, especially one who's having a bad week.

STEP 7: STAY LOYAL

Loyalty. I've mentioned this several times before because of its level of importance. Knowing that you would defend each and every team member, even if they weren't in the room, is very powerful in building trust and developing a strong bond. Be seen by other team members doing this. I also want to point out that the opposite is equally true. If you are seen to be bad-mouthing other team members to people outside the team (and inside), you'll be seen as disloyal and untrustworthy. Far better to be loyal!

Try this team culture exercise:
To get a good sense of where you are as a team member, do a simple radar chart exercise on yourself, based on the seven Team Player steps listed above. It's a good way to find your blind spots. If you're able to invite other team members to do the same thing and then share the results, so much the better.

1 Design a radar chart with your seven Team Player steps at each point around the outside edge of the chart. Now draw a straight line connecting each of them to create a heptagon. Inside this shape, draw two smaller heptagons with 0 in the centre, then 1 and 2 in the smaller heptagons and 3 in the outer shape (see diagram below).

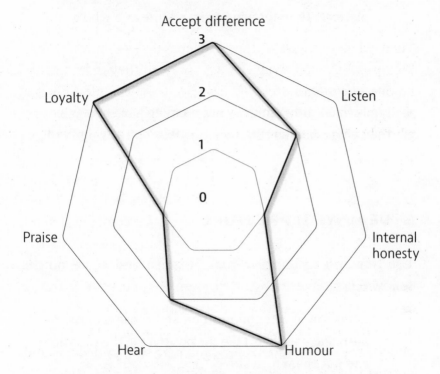

2 Complete the exercise by rating yourself from 1 to 3 for each category as a self-review against these points before joining the dots of your profile.

3 Now you can see an illustration of your strengths and weaknesses, you can begin working on them to become the best team member you can be. This diagram makes it simple to compare your

development by noting the shapes you have drawn each time you complete the test. The more regular your shape is, the more balanced your team player strengths are and, the nearer the outer heptagon you are, the better you're performing as part of a team

4   If you can involve your colleagues, suggest discussing the results at a team meeting and use this as a platform for improving team culture as a whole.

Team Culture Tip
While Hares are absolutely necessary to have because of their obvious strengths, undermanage one at your peril!

3 DEAL WITH PRESSURE

Use this drill to improve your Tortoise Test score on the following statements:

- When I'm in a tough position and those around me are being negative, I see the positives in the situation and put them forward.

- When things are becoming frustrating and I'm feeling pressure to quit, I stick with a task.

- I commit to excellence and understand that achieving it demands making tough sacrifices.

- I may move slowly, but I'm 100 per cent determined to succeed.

Pressure exists in all guises and is relative for each individual. For some people, the pressure of providing for their family by putting food on the table is just as much or more so as that experienced by a CEO who is trying to hit quarterly targets for their business. So, what is the best way to deal with it? In the same way that you would prepare for sporting competition or even a business meeting, I practise several things to get ready for the pressure around the corner.

STEP 1: DEVELOP A BULLETPROOF INTERNAL DIALOGUE

Give some thought to developing your own bulletproof internal dialogue. Write it down. Physically rehearse the words so that they're hard-wired into your mind when the pressure comes: 'I have absolute conviction that I've done my job to the best of my ability, regardless of the outcome'; 'I am good at my job'; 'Whether the result is good or bad, the process is the same, lessons will be learned and a new plan will be created'.

STEP 2: VISUALIZE SCENARIOS

If you think about your behaviour in advance, you'll want to plan for each scenario. 'How do I want to behave if X/Y/Z happens?' Visualization is well known to have many performance benefits for athletes. For example, a football player picturing themselves scoring a penalty might imagine precisely where they'll place the ball, what technique they'll use to strike it and exactly how they'll be breathing when they run up to kick the ball, even how they will celebrate. While you must do the same about your pressure situation, making sure that you prepare for both the positive and potentially negative outcomes is just as important.

STEP 3: POKER FACE

Like the swan that appears serene on the surface of the water but below is furiously paddling away, you too must develop a cool exterior no matter what is happening internally for you in a high-pressure situation. Again, the element of 'feel' comes into play here. You don't want to appear relaxed and apathetic if the occasion requires intensity, but rather focused, positive and in control, even if you don't feel that way. When you next find yourself in a moment of intense pressure, if possible prepare for it in advance and be mindful of your outward appearance. This can be as simple as monitoring how you are sitting, maintaining eye contact and not fidgeting or overly gesticulating. You may even take this as far as your breathing, keeping it slow and controlled. Like any other skill, this will take practice, but even being conscious of these things will start you down the right road.

STEP 4: PRACTISE FRAMING

Earlier in the book, I talked about different responses to threat in human behaviour such as fight or flight and I used the term 'frame'. When you are under pressure, this is the perfect time to frame the situation. Hold your position. Do nothing. Wait. Watch. Then decide your response and action. Too many people are panicked into knee-jerk reactions during highly stressful moments, which shows that the pressure has got to them and affected their performance. Practise framing and develop your confidence in holding your position. The more often you do it, the more powerful it becomes.

Try this internal dialogue exercise:
This is one of my most effective tools for dealing with tough times. Having to hand, either on my laptop or my phone, a set

Performing Under Pressure

In my job, pressure exists in the physical performance and on-court results of the player. When watching them during matches, my emotions are on a knife-edge and the adrenaline is pumping. Of course, taking the player through workouts, and making sure that they execute the movements to the best of their ability, also brings a level of pressure, especially with a high-profile athlete, but nothing beats the stress I endure when the match is taking place. That said, when warming Andy Murray up for the Wimbledon men's singles final in 2013, my nerves were jangling – the enormity of what was at stake obviously got the better of me. A part of Andy's warm-up involved me throwing tennis balls at him to work on his reactions, a routine we both knew very well. However, that day I was throwing those balls all over the place, rarely hitting the intended target. Luckily, Andy excelled under pressure and he went out and won the title. We have often joked about that warm-up since.

of affirmations that I can refer back to as an anchor to steady myself when under duress has been hugely beneficial to me.

My suggestion is to write these out during a neutral, stress-free time. It can be hard to think of positives, especially when experiencing pressure or if others are doubting you. Be as specific and as clear as possible with these notes, and write down as many as you can. You never know which sentence may strike a chord with you in a certain situation. Also ensure that you are noting things that are either facts or that you genuinely believe to be true. For example, saying to yourself,

'I'm the best at dealing with numbers and figures in my team' is not going to help you if you are clearly not that person.

These affirmations should and will change over time. You will weed out specific lines that don't help you when you read them in a state of stress. You'll also add in new attributes or achievements as they occur. Keep these notes private, for your eyes only. Colleagues and bosses must certainly not see them. They could be interpreted as boastful or even arrogant, and nobody expects you to swagger around your working environment reminding everyone of such things. They are for you to read by yourself, when times are difficult and you need to remind yourself of positive things.

Your script should contain affirmations that you're good at your job, backed up by personal reminders of your Tortoise values, with examples of when you've lived them, e.g., 'I'm never outworked by anyone' or 'I've shown fortitude by surviving restructures before'.

1   List key achievements and any success you've had.

2   List compliments, especially those given to you by mentors or managers.

3   Reaffirm good values and effort levels, such as 'I've done my job to the best of my ability, that's all anyone can ask for'; 'Maintain a positive outlook'; 'Stay objective and keep emotion out of this situation'; 'You have been given this job because someone believes in you and your ability to do it'.

4   Remind yourself that you're loved and surrounded by good people who care about you, no matter what outcomes may happen at work.

5   In a week or a month, everyone will have moved on
    to thinking about something else entirely, as will
    you. 'This moment shall pass.'

> *Pressure Tip*
> The more effort you put into preparing for stress and
> pressure, the better equipped you will be at handling it.
> This is not time wasted – it's time well invested.

4 DEAL WITH FAILURE

Use this drill to improve your Tortoise Test score on the
following statements:

- When I'm in a tough position and those around me
  are being negative, I see the positives in the situation
  and put them forward.

- When things are becoming frustrating and I'm
  feeling pressure to quit, I stick with a task.

- I may move slowly, but I'm 100 per cent determined
  to succeed.

It is now very commonly accepted that failure is not only
an inevitable part of life, but that one of the only ways we
really develop as individuals is by failing repeatedly. In fact,
we are almost going to the other end of the spectrum and
conditioning ourselves to celebrate failures because they teach
us lessons. I agree with this philosophy. That said, failure at a

task that means a lot to you feels awful. Working on a task as a team and failing feels terrible. Here are the best ways that I've learned to deal with the failures I've been involved in.

STEP 1: SHOW UP, DON'T HIDE

Be there in the locker room, in the office, show up for the meeting, be seen. Simply by being there for others and others for you, in hard times, is help enough. You don't even need to say much at all. Your physical presence is reassurance, solidarity and a great place from which to build.

STEP 2: COME BACK STRONGER

As soon as is appropriate, start the plan to come back stronger. Timing this step correctly is important – people must be allowed to mourn a loss or failure. This is where

---

Experiencing Failure

Whether on a training day aiming for a specific goal or when they compete in matches, at some point all sportsmen experience failure. Looking at the sport I work in, even the greatest tennis players of all time lose. And they lose a lot! At the time of writing, Roger Federer has won 1,242 matches (an incredible feat) but he has also lost 271 times. Serena Williams has won 834 matches and lost 144. Even though her win-to-lose ration is almost 6 to 1, there are still many failures among the triumphs. My point here is certainly not to denigrate either of these legends' careers, but simply to say that even the very best can't win all of the time. More importantly, they certainly know how to put these losses behind them, learn from them and move on. Perhaps that's ultimately why they've achieved so much.

---

developing feel for the situation is vital.

The right time to begin the plan is somewhere between strolling into the locker room and saying 'Heigh-ho, never mind, onwards and upwards' immediately after defeat, to not speaking for a week and letting negativity fester. The plan should contain answers to certain questions: 'What mistakes were made?', 'What lessons were learned?', 'Where are we weak?', 'What actually went well about the plan we had?', 'What are the consequences of this failure and how do we best go about minimizing them?' A show of Tortoise-like fortitude is the best value to display.

STEP 3: ACCEPT RESPONSIBILITY

I've always found that volunteering to accept responsibility for my mistakes can encourage others to do the same. You don't want to do this every time, however, or be the only one doing this. The best way to phrase this would be: 'Look, I've reflected on the result and I've got to hold my hands up and take responsibility for X. What do you think?'

STEP 4: ABSORB EMOTION

It's important to let people vent in a supportive environment and not immediately jump to defence mode. Just absorb the information and take it in the context in which it is said, making allowances for emotions to be high. When you think of the kind of personality traits in our Stress Buster Tortoise descriptor, this person would be calm and considered, giving an impression of experience, while pointing out a long-term or big-picture perspective.

STEP 5: EXPECT BETTER TIMES

As with pressure, know that this failure, too, shall pass. As

I said at the start, you can expect to be stronger, wiser and more prepared the next time, after a failure. Better times will be on the horizon.

Try this visualization exercise:
Say that the outcome of your Annual Performance Review is bad and you've underperformed in the past year, not meeting the standards set out by your superiors. This is what you do:

1   Show up and be present in the moment, with positive body language. Maintain eye contact with your boss, sit up straight in your chair. In the days and weeks immediately after your review, show the same positive body language and energy when going about your work. Be seen to be unaffected by the bad news and actually re-double your efforts. That's what showing up means.

2   Start the plan for improving, so that the same result does not happen next year. What additional training might you require? Can you shadow someone who is more successful in a specific facet of your work? How about setting yourself shorter-term weekly or monthly targets to hit? Suggest meeting more regularly with your boss to see how you are progressing with these.

3   Take responsibility for things that haven't gone well. This doesn't mean being submissive and apologizing for your entire year of work, but rather holding your hands up and admitting that you need to improve. Stating that you are determined to make the necessary adjustments, in a mature fashion, shows strength.

4 Listen. Allow your boss to give you the feedback without interruption. Let them vent, if necessary. Maintain that eye contact and make sure they know you are listening.

5 Know that this will pass. Whatever happens, tomorrow is another day and you'll have to get out of bed and put in your best effort, no matter what. And accept that, if you do this, better times will be ahead for you.

Failure Tip
Thinking about how failure looks and feels before it happens is a far more effective way of dealing with it than by not preparing at all and being reactive.

5 DEAL WITH SUCCESS

Use this drill to improve your Tortoise Test score on the following statements:

- I speak with conviction about subjects I really care about in all situations, be it meetings, casual conversations at lunch or phone calls to my friends.

- I can wait for the success I want, even though it's going to take a long time to reach.

- I may move slowly, but I'm 100 per cent determined to succeed.

When success comes (and it will), you must make sure you take the time to truly enjoy it in exactly the way you want to. There's nothing wrong with having a plan for this, either. How, where and with whom do you want to celebrate? Knowing the answers to these questions makes it real and exciting in your mind. Looking at pressure, failure or success, there's a pattern here. One thing's for sure: like failure, it will pass. Before you know it, the next challenge will come along. The current success will be a thing of the past, which is all the more reason to ensure you make the most of it.

STEP 1: ENJOY THE MOMENT

Enjoying the moment doesn't necessarily look like running around the room, waving your arms in the air and screaming with delight. Quite the opposite, in fact. Your body language could be similar to that of dealing with failure (sitting upright, calm with good eye contact) and, importantly, being humble. That said, you should still have in your mind how you will celebrate with family and friends later on!

STEP 2: PLAN FOR BETTER

As with dealing with pressure or indeed failure, as soon as is appropriate, start the plan for how you will go one stage better. Already having your ideas for this and not being content to sit on your laurels is certainly the right mindset here. You also have the added bonus of being successful, which means that there could be less pressure, leaving you to be a little freer in your thinking. Striking the balance between steps 1 and 2 here is the key to getting this right. All too often myself, I have either not taken the time to enjoy a triumph nor used the momentum to take advantage of one. The best will always want to get better and as is so often

Pushing For the Next Goal

I remember when Andy Murray beat Novak Djokovic to become the world number one in the very last match of 2016 at the ATP Masters Finals in London. I walked back into the locker room to find Ivan Lendl (Andy's coach and mentor) already strategizing and planning for the next season. This struck me as so impressive. Andy had just become the best player in the world and Ivan wasn't satisfied with that. Where others may have backed off after achieving an amazing goal like that, Ivan's first thoughts were of future domination and how to get better. This was a real lesson for me and an example of great leadership.

said in the world of sport, if you are not improving then you are standing still, and to stand still is to fall behind.

STEP 3: ACKNOWLEDGE OTHERS

Be humble when you achieve success. Credit is something that you should look to give, not receive. If you've done something good, people will know. Telling everyone you've done something good can have the opposite effect. Acknowledging others for the contribution they have made is far more powerful. Be specific in your praise of others who have helped you along the way, including your boss and other colleagues. You'd hope others would do this for you, so be the person that does it for them.

Try this success snowball exercise:
You'll have heard that small successes grow with a snowball-like effect. So, pick a goal right now and do five things this very

day towards achieving it, no matter how small. Then do another five tomorrow, and so on every day for an entire week. I promise you that after seven days you'll feel more confident in achieving that goal and you'll have built some momentum. More than that, you'll have felt what it's like to have some success.

Let's say you made thirty-five steps towards your goal in a week. In a month, that'll be up to 155 steps, over a year 1,825. Imagine how much mastery of that goal you would have in ten years' time. Is there any goal that you couldn't attain with that much commitment over a given period of time? Probably not. And I'd be willing to bet that high achievers make double that many good decisions per day. It's no wonder they can do great things. So, take note of every single little step towards your goal that you took each day. It could be finding the email address of someone who can help you along your way, waking up thirty minutes early to do some research, even exercising to improve your energy levels and appearance.

> *Success Tip*
> Keeping a record of your progress, and reminding yourself of how much you've done, will give you confidence and momentum.

6 PLAY TWO OR THREE MOVES AHEAD

Use this drill to improve your Tortoise Test score on the following statements:

- I recognize that generosity of spirit towards others is not only the best way to get a positive outcome in a situation, but also feels better.

- I can wait for the success I want, even though it's going to take a long time to reach.

- I play the long game because I have faith in myself to succeed.

- I'm happy to take my time winning people over and don't mind if my good work goes unnoticed and underappreciated in the beginning.

Longevity in any role depends on the ability to see what is unfolding in front of you and predict the future direction of your department or organization. This enables you to take a position that you either feel strongly about or that will increase your chances of success. You can then align yourself with key stakeholders in these situations.

STEP 1: BE WELL INFORMED

Being well informed about the internal developments within your own environment is important. This doesn't mean idle gossip, but keeping your ear to the ground for future changes, new positions or structural and management changes that may affect you.

STEP 2: BUILD RELATIONSHIPS

Building relationships with colleagues, in order to have them share key pieces of information, will also serve to help you in all manner of situations. Knowledge is power and to have the most up-to-date inside information about the latest policies, strategies and yes, even gossip, will arm you well for future situations such as structural change and promotion. Being the Tortoise in your company (trustworthy, loyal, reliable) will help with this.

STEP 3: ALIGN YOURSELF WELL

In discussions and debates, the main influencers within your space will become apparent. Some of them may be controversial and not popular with senior management. This could mean they may not last forever within your company and it may not be a good idea for you to align yourself with them as, when they go, this may leave you exposed. On the flip side of the coin, safe and steady influencers may potentially be ousted in departmental changes if they're seen as not dynamic or strong enough. Again, you may be tarred with the same brush if they move on. So, in the changing dynamics of organizational life, think carefully about which team members you support.

STEP 4: STAY CONNECTED

Being educated about your external environment, your line of work, even the party politics in your country are all important factors in understanding and predicting what is to come. Another good idea is to connect with others who work in your sector, even for rival companies, in other countries. Being as open and sharing with them as you can be, without giving away trade secrets, will also produce nuggets of information.

Try this future brainstorming exercise:
To help you to do as much as you can to prepare for the future, this exercise considers every possible scenario and

A Hare Employs a Tortoise Strategy

Boxing legend Muhammad Ali employed the Tortoise strategy of planning a few moves ahead, especially later in his career, to great effect. Before his famous 'Rumble in the Jungle' with George Foreman in Zaire in 1974, Ali had watched tapes of Foreman knocking down Joe Frazier six times to win the heavyweight title. He'd observed how Foreman often put his hands on the ropes. Ali said, 'No stamina. Wait till he hears round six, round seven, round eight!' Ali used what is now known as his 'rope-a-dope' strategy.

His first move relied on laying on the loose ropes of the ring, pulling back, evading and rolling with all of Foreman's hardest punches – in the knowledge that he had moves two and three ahead of him. Laying on the ropes himself, Ali took away Foreman's most potent weapon and succeeded in tiring him out. Later in the fight, Ali put his second move into place by countering with jabs and right leads. Ali's final move was to knock Foreman out in the eighth round. Ali obviously understood that for long-term gain he must experience short-term pain. He stuck to his strategy of playing several moves ahead with unwavering belief and achieved one of the greatest victories in boxing history.

how it may or may not play out for you. You are going to create a mind map containing all of the possible future connotations you think you may face in your workplace. Be as creative and far-fetched in your scenarios as you'd like. Make sure, once again, that this is for your eyes only.

Create four circles (or spider bodies) labelled 'Team Future', 'Department Future', 'Company Future' and

'Industry Future'. Then, one by one, add a leg of the spider by brainstorming any developments that you see happening. Here are some ideas under each heading to get you started.

Team Future: Leader promoted/quits; disenfranchised team members leave; excelling team members promoted; team friction; team expansion.

Department Future: Given more importance within the company; expansion with more opportunities; cutbacks; change of direction/emphasis on different type of work; leaders change.

Company Future: Wins/loses major new contract; receives funding boost; takes over rival firm/is taken over; change of management; structure streamlines; relocates; changes emphasis of work.

Industry Future: Becomes obsolete; embraces technological advancements; becomes internet-based; becomes vastly more in demand; global economy experiences downturn; global markets change (bull or bear markets); change of national or international government policy; becomes temporarily popular/unpopular (bubble, burst).

For each leg you give the spider, try to follow the consequences through by adding an extension to this leg and keep going until you have answered every possible connotation of each leg. If there are three possible results, then create three legs and follow each one through.

What you should end up with is a large sheet with almost every possible scenario for your future career laid out on

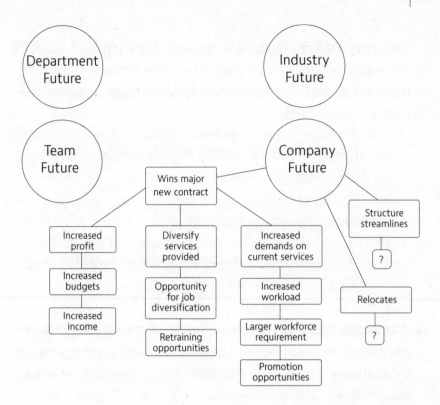

it. More importantly, you will have already spent a lot of time thinking of several moves ahead for yourself. You'll have considered the potential ripple effects of not just your own micro-environmental situation, but every conceivable circumstance in your industry.

Now, lock these scenarios into your subconscious and begin aligning yourself with the most favourable factors within your control, as well as preparing for larger future developments that may be out of your control.

Future Planning Tip
Forewarned is forearmed. Take into account every possible scenario you can imagine.

7 MANAGE CHANGE

Use this drill to improve your Tortoise Test score on the following statements:

- I play the long game because I have faith in myself to succeed.

- I commit to excellence and understand that achieving it demands making tough sacrifices.

- I work hard and am prepared to put in consistently high effort day to day.

Being the Tortoise during times of change is highly advantageous. Performing well under this stress, being seen to be strong, unwavering, positive and patient will impress. Many others will have emotional highs and lows and be reactive. Your job is to be positive and proactive. Here's my guide to how you can succeed in this respect.

The overriding rule here is to control what you can control. There will be many things that you won't have any control over, mainly decisions and other people's reactions. In Chapter Four, I talked about the power of holding your position, and this certainly applies when managing change. Everything here is focused on not reacting, not showing your hand, but keeping your poker face and waiting.

Hopefully, you will have seen the change coming and aligned yourself with the best possible stakeholders. Should the changes affect you directly, you'll also have contacts in the wider environment of your sector to turn to for a back-up plan. During this time, this preparation gives you that all-important position of strength that you always want to have.

STEP 1: STAY POSITIVE

You absolutely must keep a positive frame of mind. So, embrace the change and see the opportunities it presents. Go with the flow rather than being resistant to it and you'll come out the other side better for the experience, no matter what the outcome.

STEP 2: ACT STRATEGICALLY

If you're in a position of responsibility, particularly a middle-management role, you must be strategically very smart. Before offering any opinions or suggestions on a restructure, wait to be told from above what is happening. Be aware that decisions may already have been made and laying your cards on the table may weaken your position.

STEP 3: THINK BUSINESS

If asked your view by those above you, make suggestions that are best for the business, not for yourself. If your ideas or advice point to you getting a huge promotion, then your view will be disregarded and, again, your position weakened.

STEP 4: CHOOSE WISELY

Be honest, but pick your battles wisely, choosing only to engage in conflict where you have a genuine belief that the wrong direction is being taken. For example, if you feel that a specific conversation relates directly to losing your job, then be as objective, reasoned and passionate as possible. In the long run, you will ultimately save your job in other ways by displaying these qualities.

STEP 5: MANAGE MINDSET

When communicating down to those you manage, try to

Change is Good

During my time with the Lawn Tennis Association, the governing body of UK tennis, I experienced two complete regime changes through different CEOs. Along with that came restructure and a change of middle management. In this time, I twice moved location for my job and went on to work with many different colleagues, not to mention players. Leaving the group of young teenage players whom I'd been developing for five years at a performance academy is still one of the most heart-wrenching experiences of my professional career.

Over a decade of employment, I went from being a sports governing body's entry-level strength and conditioning (S&C) coach to leading the department of coaches nationally. During my time with Andy Murray, I've worked with around fifteen different performance team members, including four 'super coaches' and three day-to-day coaches, all of whom operate differently and approach the game in their own unique ways. Again, I've gone from a pro player's entry-level S&C coach, assisting Jez Green, to a leading member of Andy's performance support team. As I was working for both employers at the same time for around seven of those years, much of this change was overlapping. I had to reapply for my job once and survive a reshuffle the second time around. Without doubt, these were stressful times, but all of them led to better outcomes for me in the long run.

spend time with your team. This means being seen and conveying constant positivity. Make no promises that you can't keep, say nothing negative about the new structure, express no fears or doubts of your own. Do a lot of listening, allowing people to vent to you without judging them and providing a safe place for their concerns. Where possible, being seen to address these concerns is important for morale. Most importantly, prepare them for the change with the correct mindset. Speculation will be rife. Accept this as a normal part of the process, but discourage it and certainly don't join in.

Try this change exercise:
While there are many ways to get your team to think about change, I find this one works quickly and can be done as part of a regular catch-up meeting.

1   At the start of the meeting, simply instruct everyone to fold their arms until you tell them to stop. Then just carry on the meeting as normal.

2   After five minutes or so, stop talking and ask people to uncross their arms and re-cross them the opposite way.

3   The likely result is a lot of fumbling, as most of the team struggle with what should seem a simple physical exercise.

4   Use the perplexity and laughter to generate a conversation about change. Start by asking how it felt when you asked them to cross their arms the other way. Did it come naturally to them or did they struggle and have to think about it?

5   Move on to other questions: Were they comfortable trying a different approach? If this is one thing that makes them resistant to change, are there others?

Change Tip
Change is inevitable. It's the only constant. Stay positive and act strategically.

---

8 MANAGE CONFLICT

Use this drill to improve your Tortoise Test score on the following statements:

- I stand up for work colleagues if they aren't in the room and someone else is saying negative things about them.

- When I'm in a tough position and those around me are being negative, I see the positives in the situation and put them forward.

- When things are becoming frustrating and I'm feeling pressure to quit, I stick with a task.

I have to admit, conflict is my least favourite aspect of life, albeit an occasionally necessary one. To me, there are two kinds: premeditated and unexpected. The first can happen in a couple of ways – when you must confront a person and air a grievance, or when you are asked to meet with someone who is airing a grievance. What they have in common is that you know both of these situations are going to happen in advance. Secondly, there's the type of conflict that comes out of the blue, which you must simply react to in the moment. This could be a car accident or an argument in a team meeting. Completely unexpected. Roads, car parks, supermarkets, public transport, bars, meetings and now social media are all common ground for this kind of dispute.

STEP 1: VISUALIZE RESOLUTION

In any type of confrontation, it's important to minimize the emotional aspect. One way to do this is imagine (both beforehand and even during the actual situation) that you're viewing the scene from a fly-on-the-wall or third-person perspective. Visualize the room, looking down on the debate from the ceiling, or even picturing two of your friends having the exact same argument. Then, think about being the mediator between those people in the room. What would you say to them? What would be the fairest outcome? In which aspects do they both have salient points to make? What direction would you not want this conflict to go in? What kind of statements should neither person make and which subjects are off-limits here?

STEP 2: MIND THE LANGUAGE

Prepare for the kind of body language, tone of voice and even level of self-restraint that you must exercise. Do this by watching clips of how others have dealt well with confrontation, e.g. police and other emergency services doing their jobs, even professional bouncers in bars and nightclubs. Bailiffs, debt collectors, parking wardens all have to manage conflict on an hourly basis in their working lives, so observe them and then practise mimicking their responses, but adding your situation to the language.

STEP 3: BUY TIME AND REMOVE THE STING

Upon initial contact, listen calmly and validate what the person is saying by making a comment like, 'Yes, I can see your perspective here.' Don't interrupt them, just listen until they have finished. If they have some valid points in their argument, it may save you time and aggravation to simply acknowledge them, apologize and thank them for their feedback. This will obviously not be the solution every time, but it will not hurt to try it occasionally.

STEP 4: ADDRESS SPECIFICS

Once you've validated the other person's emotion and let them get everything off their chest, you can go about addressing each point in a methodical way. When others are listing their issues, especially in an emotive way, they will often leave what is really underneath it all until the very last point, so make sure you let them get there. Take note of key words and phrases they use in their argument. Quoting these back to them will show that you are both listening and understanding their points. Mirroring and matching body language and tone of voice will also help here.

STEP 5: COMPROMISE WHERE APPROPRIATE

Although most conflict is born out of opposing views or clashing values, I've most often found that the answer lies somewhere in the middle. Trying to find common ground to move forward is the only way out – but, of course, both parties must have a level of willingness to do this. Just because the situation is challenging you, make sure that you do not commit to something you don't agree with, especially in the work setting. Promise only to treat each issue with care and to follow through by examining each one. Setting a

Unexpected Conflict

In my younger days as a strength and conditioning coach, I came across one of the junior players I worked with who was crying in the corridor of the tennis centre. When I asked what the problem was, they told me that they'd had enough of the lifestyle, the pressure and the sheer difficulty of training to be a world-class tennis player, and that they wanted to quit. The player then went on to say that they were really nervous about talking to their parents about it. I naturally wanted to help the young person and volunteered to mediate at a meeting between the player and their parents later that evening. I thought that the parents would simply acquiesce to their child's despair and agree. I was wrong.

When the conversation started, the parents were very angry about all the money they had ploughed into their child's training. They had sacrificed a lot and were not about to let this career be dropped on a whim. As the mediator in the room, I completely froze. I was totally unprepared for this to turn into a conflict. The player was looking to me for help and support, and I gave none. Fortunately, a far more experienced colleague of mine walked past the meeting room and saw the scene that was unfolding. They must have also noticed the lost look on my face and came to the rescue. The meeting was calmly broken up and we agreed for the player to take a few days' rest and return to speak to the head coaches when the dust had settled. This meeting has stayed with me ever since – I realized then how pivotal it was to be prepared for conflict to develop in certain situations and to always have a plan to deal with that eventuality.

realistic time frame to get back to the person is the correct resolution. Finally, make sure you do this, or expect a doubly difficult conversation next time.

Try these conflict preparation exercises:
The only way to get better at holding your position and dealing with conflict is to get out of your comfort zone and practise these stages. Generating conflict is not what I am advocating. However, seeking out current situations in your life with unresolved issues is a good start. In either of the premeditated circumstances, you want to be as prepared as possible. Although unpleasant, this means thinking about conflict in advance.

Scenario 1: Confronting someone yourself

→ Pick a situation in which you're unhappy, but haven't yet managed to say to someone what you'd like.

→ Plan your approach in terms of what you will say and how you will say it.

→ Acknowledge feelings of nerves, or even anger, if you're particularly aggrieved.

→ Think of the words you have listed above and talk yourself into 'feeling' and acting this way, e.g. 'I want to feel professional and fair', 'I will act in a calm and considered way'.

→ Visualize yourself leading with objectivity rather than emotion, or the conflict may not be as productive as you hope.

→ Set a goal for what you'd ideally like to achieve, as well as a bare minimum that you must walk away with.

→ Finally, gather as much fact-based evidence in order to back up your points – if the confrontation turns into an argument, you must rely on these to remain objective.

Scenario 2: Being confronted by someone

→ Take an area of your life where you're likely to have some form of disagreement soon.

→ Realize that the colleague you have in mind may approach you first, in which case you're less likely to have prepared specifically for what they may throw at you.

→ Hopefully, however, you will have a good feel for your working environment and be able to play two or three moves ahead.

→ If you can predict potential conflict with this colleague, why not engage Scenario 1 as quickly as possible, so that you are on the front foot and not being reactive?

Whatever your scenario, the overriding question to yourself should be 'How do I want to behave during this confrontation to reach an outcome whereby both parties can move forward in an amicable way?' Words like 'calm', 'considered', 'fair', 'assertive' and 'professional' occur to me here. Choose some words which resonate with you. If you can't do any of this, think back to previous situations you've faced and how they might have turned out for the better if you'd applied these principles. Probably the most important point in either scenario, though, is buying time and removing the sting, all while maintaining poise and composure. You will be able to repeat the five stages reactively, on the spot.

> **Conflict Tip**
> The more practised you are at planned conflict, the better equipped you will be at the unplanned version.

9 TAKE YOUR JOB SERIOUSLY, BUT NOT YOURSELF

Use this drill to improve your Tortoise Test score on the following statements:

- I stand up for work colleagues if they aren't in the room and someone else is saying negative things about them.

- I can wait for the success I want, even though it's going to take a long time to reach.

- When things are becoming frustrating and I'm feeling pressure to quit, I stick with a task.

- Even in the darkest of days, I retain the courage of my convictions and remain purposeful.

- I can be trusted to achieve any task that I'm set to very high standards.

- I'm happy to take my time winning people over and don't mind if my good work goes unnoticed and underappreciated in the beginning.

There's a real balance to be struck here. People who take themselves too seriously can often be irritating to others and alienate themselves. People who aren't serious enough don't develop credibility. In my experience, one of the hardest aspects of the transition to middle management for many is being taken more seriously by peers and colleagues, when you're still viewed as the less experienced junior person. Generally speaking, as a younger professional you also tend to have a more light-hearted approach and can be the butt of office jokes as the new kid on the block. This informal initiation is commonplace in most industries. As we'll see in the next chapter on soft skills for different career levels, this is fine within reason. Everyone goes through it. Just try to have fun with it and be patient like the Tortoise. Here are some steps to achieve this balance in behaviour at different stages in your career.

BEHAVIOURAL BALANCE STEPS FOR ENTRY LEVEL

Step 1: Time and experience will gain you respect, so be as good at your job as possible. People generally make fun of you as a way of breaking down formal barriers and creating a connection with you. Denying them this opportunity will also deny that connection, which doesn't bode well for working as part of a team.

Step 2: Develop an awareness of the sinister side of workplace banter. There may be those in your environment who purposely belittle other team members in order to heighten or maintain their own standing within the pecking order. Counter this by making sure that, when discussing work topics, you show your serious side. Be firm, considered and accurate in what you say.

Step 3: When talking about yourself and subjects about you, have a sense of humour. The ability to laugh at yourself is highly underrated and will endear you to workmates. But avoid doing this when talking about work, because you risk making a joke out of it.

BEHAVIOURAL BALANCE STEPS FOR MIDDLE MANAGERS

Step 1: It can be good to be seen as self-effacing. Staff will respond well to a certain degree of informal connection. As you must initially establish respect, this informal bridge-building is second on the priority list to developing mutually respectful working relationships with the team.

Step 2: Watch out for negative banter towards colleagues. Some may feel threatened by new staff with new ideas, who may climb the ladder faster. They use put-downs as a means of pigeon-holing people, with the ultimate goal of devaluing their position. Taking a strong stand is necessary somewhere along the line. While leaders must never be clowns, showing your human side at the right time and in the right place can help your team's morale.

Step 3: Be mindful that subordinates may regularly try to engage you in informal conversation to create a bond that may influence decision-making or curry favour.

BEHAVIOURAL BALANCE STEPS FOR SENIOR MANAGERS

Step 1: Your position may involve making redundancies or dealing with disciplinary issues, so your staff need to know that you can crack the whip on occasion. If people in your team feel you are a pushover because you get too close or aren't serious enough, you will come under a great deal of pressure. This can be a very difficult position to rescue. Better to start strict and then ease off, than start soft and try to build respect.

Some Things I've Done . . .

To make you feel better about taking yourself out of your comfort zone, here are just some of the things I've ended up doing under the guise of not taking myself too seriously:

- singing without prior warning at an official dinner, with royalty present;

- wearing a pink velour training kit for a week to training and dinner, as well as being called onto court wearing this outfit at an exhibition match with thousands watching

- performed an aerobics routine to 300 staff at an all-colleague day;

- disco-danced for sixty seconds to no music in front of tennis fans waiting for autographs;

- subjected myself to a naked ice bath ...

So how do you recover from this to ever be taken seriously? The answer is a simple rule: when talking about yourself, smiley face. When talking shop, game face.

Step 2: If your work or your ideas are regularly the subject of humour and laughed at, then put a stop to this immediately by either refusing to engage or certainly no longer joining in. Being seen to have a sense of humour failure about it and pushing back occasionally will redress the balance.

Try this working relationships exercise:
This will help you to think about these relationships and form some decisions on whether or not you need to make any adjustments to them.

Make a list of all colleagues you interact with on a regular basis and grade your relationship with them. Then start to look for trends. We start with a relationship assessment scale of 1 to 5:

1   Very formal, only ever discuss work topics. Humour is never used in conversations.

2   Formal, very occasional reference to personal lives and use of humour, but mostly work is discussed.

3   Balanced, polite and respectfully formal when required, but also an ease of communication and fun when appropriate.

4   Informal, primarily discussing non-work-related subjects. A level of awkwardness around formal subjects.

5   Very informal, almost never discuss work subjects. Primary interaction is around fun and humour. Difficult to actually be serious.

Entry-level employee? You may have a higher proportion of relationships that are a 3+. This is the nature of your daily interaction as well as, probably, your outlook in life. Your relationship with any senior figure is closer to a 1 or 2, but with your peers 4 or 5.

Middle manager? I'd expect that more of your relationships are 3–. With your peers, they could be a 3 or possibly a 4 for those whom you know well and trust. With your team, they could be anywhere from 1 to 3. With senior management, a 1 or 2.

Senior manager? My expectation is that most of your relationships in the workplace are 1 or 2.

These are by no means rules. Quite the opposite. This exercise is simply designed to make you think about these interpersonal relationships and manage them more on your terms. Design a profile of relationships that you desire, not one that is imposed on you by others in your environment. If some of your workplace relationships are not where you'd like them to be, set yourself a goal of at least a month and gradually change your behaviours around that person over time.

Seriousness Tip
Extreme behaviour changes will just seem strange and likely spoil your connection. As always, Tortoise-paced changes are the best and most likely to last.

10 WORK WELL WITH SUCCESSFUL HIGH ACHIEVERS

Use this drill to improve your Tortoise Test score on the following statements:

- I commit to excellence and understand that achieving it demands making tough sacrifices.

- I can be trusted to achieve any task that I'm set to very high standards.

As you climb the ladder of success, you will come into contact with and probably work for an industry influencer, a powerful individual in your particular field. I have come across many and I'm going to offer my seven rules of engagement for how best to deal with them.

Firstly, however, to set the scene, I want to share my personal experiences of being around elite sportspeople. What separates the highly successful from those who are less so? For me, it's because they constantly take the following steps:

STEP 1: BE DEDICATED

Little things add up. There are literally hundreds of decisions we make every single day, from what time to wake up to what to eat for breakfast, choosing the first task of the working day and so on. It's perfecting these personal choices every day that makes the difference. The highest achievers get the vast majority of these decisions right. And their accumulation builds momentum, huge confidence and success. For an athlete, it's the discipline of habits – eating, sleeping, exercise, training, sacrifice, travelling to anywhere necessary for whatever length of time it takes. For an entrepreneur, it's spending every waking moment thinking about their product, researching, networking with buyers, finding the best and learning from them. The exciting thing about this discipline is that it's controllable and, therefore, achievable by anyone who has the determination.

STEP 2: WORK HARDER THAN EVERYONE ELSE

Another commitment of the highest achievers is to never be outworked and never to compromise. They are often described as having an 'obsession'. One athlete I know thinks 'obsession' is a word that the less committed, the less disciplined and the less hard-working use to justify their own relative shortcomings in this area. You don't have to be obsessed to work harder and be more committed than everyone else. High achievers are single-minded in their approach, so nothing stops them from pushing themselves every single day to the limits of either their mental capacity or physical ability. You can see how these people generate massive change and become forces to be reckoned with.

STEP 3: BE COMPETITIVE

Almost without exception, high achievers are incredibly competitive about everything in their field. Although this isn't confined exclusively to their working life. Most of them would fight tooth and nail over a game of tiddlywinks! High achievers also hate to lose more than they love to win, which makes being around them after a failure or loss an even more intense experience.

Daily Excellence

While preparing for a role in the movie *Mile 22*, actor Mark Wahlberg revealed his daily routine on Instagram. This highlights perfectly the points made above regarding little decisions and extraordinary dedication:

2.30 a.m.	Wake up
2.45 a.m.	Prayer time
3.15 a.m.	Breakfast
3.40–5.15 a.m.	Workout
5.30 a.m.	Post-workout meal
6.00 a.m.	Shower
7.30 a.m.	Golf
8.00 a.m.	Snack
9.30 a.m.	Cryo chamber recovery
10.30 a.m.	Snack
11.00 a.m.	Family time/meetings/work calls
1.00 p.m.	Lunch
2.00 p.m.	Meetings/work calls
3.00 p.m.	Pick up kids from school
3.30 p.m.	Snack
4.00 p.m.	Workout number 2
5.00 p.m.	Shower
5.30 p.m.	Dinner/family time
7.30 p.m.	Bedtime

As you can see, this gruelling regimen includes two workouts and seven meals every single day, as well as setting aside time for other work-related issues, family time and even thirty minutes for hitting a few golf balls. Wahlberg did this for forty-seven days, including during his family holiday and when working away from home. The results of this kind of sacrifice are there for all to see. In 2017, he was named Hollywood's highest-paid actor.

STEP 4: BELIEVE IN YOURSELF

Another common denominator with such individuals is a deep level of self-belief. Even if this isn't apparent on a superficial level, they will quietly (or loudly) believe they are the best. Is this self-belief something they are born with? Is it a personality trait? No. This self-belief is earned. They've done the work, they've made the sacrifices, they've earned the victories.

STEP 5: USE PRESSURE TO YOUR ADVANTAGE

Pressure makes diamonds. The most exciting and inspiring moments to be around high achievers are when the pressure is at its absolute highest. They raise their intensity. They continue to perform to their own very high level where others capitulate. They even actually improve. They thrive on it. Pick any one of the best individuals in the world and watch them operate when their back is against the wall and the heat is on. That's when the magic happens!

STEP 6: BE YOURSELF

High achievers are inspirational just by being themselves. These individuals have an energy, an aura that surrounds them, which is infectious. Their confidence, self-assuredness, passion and authority all rub off on everyone around them. This influence can swing hugely in a positive or negative way, depending on their own emotional state of mind.

Now you know something about what drives the highly successful, here are seven practical rules to bear in mind before you meet one:

1 DO THE MINIMUM

Successful people are constantly approached by people who want something from them. Be different. Be polite and minimalistic. The first and most important rule is to take the less is more approach. This is very much a Tortoise concept. Take your time to build a connection with a high achiever – through a drip, drip method of communication, not an opening of the floodgates! Remember my first contact with Andy Murray? I simply introduced myself and said, 'If there's anything you need, I'm around'. Then I left him alone.

2 LISTEN

Just as importantly, listen. Spend most of your time doing just that. While a high achiever will eventually want to get to know you, it is far more important to them that you get to know them and what makes them tick.

3 PROVE YOUR WORTH

In the initial stage of building a relationship with a high-achieving individual, you must prove your trustworthiness. So, do exactly what they tell you to do (within reason, of course) in exactly the way they want you to do it. Be reliable, simply get on with the task without asking too many questions to clarify. If they are an Alpha Hare, they won't have much patience and will be quick to judge you negatively.

4 ASK QUESTIONS

In time, you will prove your worthiness and trust, and then you can begin trying to assert some of your influence upon this person's thinking. However, when you do get your chance, should you just tell them, straight up, how you think the world should run? Nope. This individual has built their own success and has strong views on how to achieve it. You will negatively impact your credibility and possibly alienate yourself. The key to influencing them is to ask questions that elicit the right answers rather than telling them. Make them think that an idea is theirs by first planting it, subtly dropping in supporting information over a few days/weeks and letting it sink in. Then wait, with Tortoise-like patience. It could be a week, a month or even a year down the line, but they will get it.

5 CREATE RESPECT

If, on the rare occasion, you must disagree with a high achiever, make sure you are correct and have plenty of evidence to support your claims. You may well have to back down and concede the debate, but you will have made your point and hopefully have built some mutual respect in the process.

6 ABSORB EMOTION

In bad times, let them vent. Once again, listen and try your best to address any valid issues raised. Much of the time, simply allowing them to get their frustrations off their chest can make a big difference.

7 STAY HUMBLE

In good times, let it be about them. Be humble and have a low ego like the Tortoise. Allow the high achiever all the plaudits and seek no attention for yourself. Trying to steal the thunder of this type of person never ends well.

Try this high achiever exercise:
I want you to pick out one highly successful person. They can be in your chosen field of expertise, or simply operate within an area of interest to you. They could even be

associated with something completely unrelated to you – you simply respect them as a legend or icon in the world. Your task is to get to know them. Not in a literal sense, but metaphorically, studying everything about them. There'll be plenty written about them and online footage. What I'm particularly interested in is not so much watching them in action, but discovering which habits have made them a success. Take detailed notes and quotes on:

→ little daily decisions they get right;

→ how they display more dedication than everyone else;

→ their daily routine;

→ their competitiveness;

→ how they talk about themselves in terms of their self-belief;

→ their behaviour when under pressure and how they respond;

→ their body language, their laser-like focus and reactions;

→ their energy, their aura, their passion for what they do;

→ how they have inspired others around them – teammates, other competition, family, etc.

Once you've done this, take a look at your notes and see how many things you can apply to yourself. The notes you've taken aren't really about this person's results, more about their behaviours. What is stopping you from adopting every single one of these behaviours? Which behaviours of yours are currently at or close to replicating theirs?

High Achiever Tip

The only things stopping you from working well with a high achiever are energy and discipline. There are numerous mini windows of opportunity in your day for you to implement your 'success snowball' – make this time.

11 LEAD BY TAKING ACTION

Use this drill to improve your Tortoise Test score on the following statements:

- I play the long game because I have faith in myself to succeed.

- When given a job to do, I simply get on with it and keep going until the task is complete.

- I'm happy to take my time winning people over and don't mind if my good work goes unnoticed and underappreciated in the beginning.

I have come to realize that those who are presented with a problem and leap into action, putting a plan into place and taking immediate steps – whether the actions are making phone calls, pulling in favours, drawing upon contacts, internet searching and hustling others for potential solutions

– are actually quite rare. Such people know that sitting around just talking about the problem, or being affected by the 'Yeah, but' mentality of others who find any reason to avoid doing something, is not leadership. As a former colleague and mentor of mine used to say, 'After all is said and done, there is more said than done!'

This is where you, as a Tortoise, can be a leader without actually being appointed as one. Taking the initiative and finding solutions without being asked forges a path for others to watch and to follow. Doing this often enough, when issues arise within a team, can lead to promotion, because you have already stepped up to adopt leadership behaviours.

There are no steps to think about in this section. Instead, just roll up your sleeves and try this quick action exercise:

1   Find an appropriate task, leap into it with a surge of energy.

2   For once, I don't want you to have much of a plan of action. Instead, simply think about what can be done instantly to start solving the problem and finishing the task. Then, just do it.

3   As you delve deeper, other solutions (and new problems) will appear. Just be reactive and solve them as you go.

4   On this occasion, don't look too far ahead – take things as they come and just go for it. You'll be surprised at how quickly you can achieve progress and how good it makes you feel.

If you jump in and take the lead on a task that has already been singled out as a priority and which everyone is already working hard on, this could be seen as one-upmanship on your part – trying to win favour with management or just plain stepping on others' toes. Instead, focus on a task that has either been forgotten about, left by the wayside or simply isn't a team priority. It may even be a job that no one else wants to do.

> *Action Leading Tip*
> Be a doer, not a passenger. Show Tortoise-like consistently high effort and lead from the front.

12 TAKE CARE OF YOURSELF, FAMILY AND LOVED ONES

Use this drill to improve your Tortoise Test score on the following statements:

- I speak with conviction about subjects I really care about in all situations, be it meetings, casual conversations at lunch or phone calls to my friends.

- When things are becoming frustrating and I'm feeling pressure to quit, I stick with a task.

- Even in the darkest of days, I retain the courage of my convictions and remain purposeful.

- When given a job to do, I simply get on with it and keep going until the task is complete.

- I can be trusted to achieve any task that I'm set to very high standards.

While finding the right work/life balance is something that is talked about constantly among work colleagues, many high achievers struggle in this area. This is certainly the case when you are climbing the ladder. The levels of commitment, work ethic and sacrifice are simply too high to be able to devote enough time to family, friends and loved ones. This, in turn, requires even more care and thought over time spent with them in order to make it of the highest quality possible.

As with your career, as much effort and commitment as you can afford must go towards staying connected to your family and friends. Unaddressed imbalances here can lead

Small Changes, Big Difference

One of the issues currently facing global ecology has been the amount of plastic waste being dumped into the oceans. Millions of tonnes are currently floating in our seas and killing marine wildlife. Rather than wait for someone else to do something, surfer Pete Ceglinski created an invention called the Seabin. This innovative contraption sits on the surface of the sea and simply passes water through a hole in the top and through the bin. A filter catches plastic, oil and other floating debris. It's a very simple device and cost-effective, too. Ceglinski's company released a video of the Seabin in action that went viral, making the news all over the globe. Now, Seabins are expected to collect 5 tonnes of marine litter per month. What a huge difference one person can make when leading by taking action.

to losing exactly that – your connection. You must work doubly hard to re-establish this when you are at home. Neglecting this aspect of your life will inevitably end up being a regret. Achievements are so much less without someone to share them with and their support for your career will be invaluable. No man (or woman) is an island, and everyone needs friends, family and loved ones.

Of course, the larger your support network is, the greater the pressure is on you to give your time to all of them. As this can feel overwhelming, it's so important to take care of yourself, too. There is only so much you are physically capable of giving. Over the past twenty years, my job has taken me away from my family and friends a lot, and in this time I've developed strategies. I haven't always been able to live up to these guidelines, but whenever I haven't, I've certainly regretted it.

STEP 1: OVER-COMMUNICATE

Simply increasing the amount you communicate will have an impact. This requires Tortoise-like, constant high effort and takes a great deal of time. You do have enough time, you just need to use it! On the train or having lunch? Use the time you'd be spending messing around on social media to reach out to these people, rather than looking at pictures of what your friends ate for dinner.

STEP 2: BE PRESENT

When you have time to be with loved ones, try to be as focused on them as possible. Be energized at dinner time, help your kids with their homework or organize a date night with your partner. But, most importantly, be present. Being present means actively listening, retaining information, and being thoughtful and responsive to what your family and friends need.

Set rules (that apply to everyone in your household) about the use of electronics. For example, no phones at the dinner table, no electronic devices after 9 p.m. Have the conversation with your family about the need to be accessible to work colleagues during antisocial hours and how they would prefer that to be managed. Every single one of these events are opportunities to show you either care or are too busy. Don't trivialize them. Even if you have understanding loved ones, showing them that these things are important to you is the message you have to convey.

STEP 3: HAVE A PLAN

Another strategy is to always have holidays or special occasions planned for you all to look forward to. This is especially important when you travel a great deal. The first thing this does is to guarantee that you will actually spend time together, which can be the biggest challenge. During a very busy spell or when you're out on a long trip, it also gives you hope and lifts you up. While it may not completely redress the work/life balance, it really does go a long way towards improving it.

STEP 4: ABSORB

Accept that those close to you will sometimes be frustrated or angry with your job at times. Don't fight them on this or resist, because they have a right to feel this way. Even though you are also right, you are hurting their feelings. But this is where that Tortoise mentality of having a long-term perspective is important. You know deep down that the reason you are having to make sacrifices will ultimately benefit everyone around you. Accept their emotional reaction, while being kind to yourself and maintaining perspective.

Try this care exercise:
This one first requires honesty from you, then the patience and truth from family and friends you'd like to do it with you. It's the nearest you're going to get to a 360-degree review of your personal approach to taking care of your family and loved ones.

1   First, reflect on the four care steps above, then score yourself against each one, with 5 as your best mark and 1 your worst.

2   Next, select some people close to you who are going to be gentle but honest – bearing in mind that this isn't appropriate for everybody.

3   Talk them through what you intend to do and set a time to do it with them.

4   When it's convenient, sit down with them, describe the care rules, then ask them to score you honestly.

5   Compare your scores with theirs and use this to improve your approach.

Care Tip
Do everything within your power to ensure that those around you feel loved, appreciated, noticed and respected.

DRILLS AND SOFT SKILLS

- Making an assumption about what someone else wants rarely works out. Listen to the person first.

- While Hares are absolutely necessary to have because of their obvious strengths, undermanage one at your peril!

- The more effort you put into preparing for pressure and conflict, the better equipped you will be at handling it.

- Keeping a record of your progress, and reminding yourself of how much you've done, will give you confidence and momentum.

- Change is inevitable. It's the only constant. Stay positive and act strategically.

- Extreme behaviour changes will just seem strange and likely spoil your relationships. As always, Tortoise-paced changes are the best and most likely to last.

- Be a doer, not a passenger. Show Tortoise-like consistently high effort and lead from the front.

- Do everything within your power to ensure that those around you feel loved, appreciated and respected.

6

OPTIMIZING YOUR TORTOISE STRENGTHS

By now, you'll have a good idea of which type of Tortoise you most resemble and the developmental level you've reached as a Tortoise to date. To win the race, you need to apply your personal Tortoise strengths in relevant and appropriate ways, depending on where you're at in your career. However advanced you are as a Tortoise, it is crucial to be honest and humble at each career stage you attain. Getting this wrong is likely to agitate co-workers, be they above, below or in parity with you. Indeed, a common mistake shown by those starting out in their careers is to overinflate their level of experience as they seek to impress senior staff who have seen it all before, can easily spot it and will pick it apart.

To help you to apply what you now know about being a Tortoise, let's use this chapter to explore career stages in a very broad sense. I'm using my own as practical experience. Even if you've yet to reach certain levels in your chosen profession, or have passed a couple by, it's worth spending time here for insights into the mindset and soft skills of colleagues at different phases of their professional lives.

Over the next few pages, then, we'll look in detail at three career stages:

→ Pre-entry (post-graduation)

→ Entry (0–10 years)

→ Senior practitioner/middle manager (10–20 years)

There is a fourth stage, the highest of all – upper management influencer (20+ years), but I'm going to leave this out. By this point in your career, you'll have very established belief systems and behaviour patterns, and be exceptionally well entrenched in your identity. Any changes required would be highly individual and bespoke for you. Instead, I'm going to focus here on the first three. As you'd expect, each stage becomes a little more involved and detailed as you progress in your career, so expect more information at each level.

Throughout, I'll include some personal case studies, illustrating ups and downs, dos and don'ts. There'll be developmental exercises for you to try along the way and some good practice tips. In particular, I'm going to focus on how to communicate up, across and down to people at each point of your career. Last but not least, I'm going to go into the nitty gritty of three different phases within each stage: honeymoon, consolidation and challenge.

PRE-ENTRY (POST-GRADUATION)

You've decided on your dream career. This stage can start as early or as late as you want. It could be after leaving school or university, but may also apply to someone older who is changing career.

The key elements of this crucial time are your positive energy, enthusiasm and refusal to take no for an answer. You're trying to get on the first rung of the ladder, so you must knock on as many doors as possible. If you have contacts, friends of friends or even family members who know someone in your chosen profession, it's time to call upon them. The primary objective when reaching out to people is to get the tone of your communication right. Yes, you need the persistence to get noticed, but you also need subtlety and tact.

The following practice is the one I've used time and again to generate opportunities. To get it right, you have to stick at it.

GET YOUR FOOT IN THE DOOR

1. **Think.** Write down your dream job and your dream life. Be specific and ambitious.

2. **Note.** Here's the most important part – identify the best practitioners in the world, within the field you've chosen. Write down the company and contact details of these people.

3. **Act.** Begin contacting these companies and individuals, asking to simply shadow or watch them in action. Go to great lengths to explain that you can just be around for an hour or two if that's easier, and will simply stay in the background and observe.

4. **Repeat.** Write to them again – it's unlikely they will reply the first time.

5. **Relocate.** Travel to where they are based. Especially if many are located in the same region or even country. Find any paid work in that area and spend your spare time shadowing. Needing to earn money, as well as seeking to volunteer for these companies,

makes this one of the hardest working stages of your career.

6   **Volunteer.** Once you've built a small relationship, offer to undertake some menial tasks, volunteering your time. Do these jobs well.

7   **Persist.** Run through all these steps again until you have the voluntary experience and know how to attain an entry-level job at a company within your chosen field – especially an organization that can put you on the first step of the ladder to achieving your dream.

When I talk about being fully committed, this is exactly where it begins. Right here, in this early stage of your career. When I travelled from the UK to Australia to get voluntary experience, I was quite literally putting my 'foot in the door' and it really worked for me. I simply would not be where I am today if I hadn't started with this method at that specific time in my life.

NOW YOU DO IT

Pre-entry is such an exciting period. Good luck – your journey of discovery starts here:

- It's time to drop everything and find the best.

- Show consistent high effort and persistence – not only to get a foot in the door, but also to be impressive enough to be invited back.

- Remain humble and blend into the background. Do not ask hundreds of questions each time you're invited to shadow someone, but do have one or two good ones ready, in case you're asked. Once the session is finished, be polite, thank them. Mention that if there was an opportunity to revisit them in the future, you would love to, then leave.

- When you do get invited back, behave in precisely the same way. Add value, not burden.

ENTRY LEVEL (0–10 YEARS)

Finally, you now have your foot on the first rung of the ladder in your chosen career. Think about it – you've volunteered, hustled, pulled in every contact you have, including those in your soft network of family, friends and friends of friends. You've landed your first paid job.

I know that ten years seems like a very long time to feel like a beginner, or an entry-level employee, but there's a good reason for this. It's the most vital stage in your success – it's your foundation, where you form your values, learn the most and build your professional demeanour. This is also the point in your career, of course, when you make the most mistakes. That's ok, but it's important here that you don't try to cover any of them up. However it may feel at the time, it's always far better to hold your hands up and admit where you've gone wrong. Management will respect this and will probably know you made the blunder anyway. Trying to hide mistakes or denying them will badly affect people's trust in you and create far more problems down the line. I witness so many entry-level staff around me making this error and it's terrible to see.

WATCH, LISTEN AND LEARN

I've talked at length about being an enthusiastic observer when you're trying to get on the career ladder. But what about when you're finally on it? Throughout your professional life, your skills of observation will be of huge importance – never more so than when you're first starting out.

What you're most likely to be drawn to observing are the hard skills of your peers. The job itself, the organization, the wider industry and the little ways you can get ahead. But, in fact, these are not the most pivotal things to which you should be paying attention. At entry level, you should be putting more energy into monitoring the soft skills of mentors and of senior people within your organization and your industry. Although the knowledge and hard skills related to your role will be relatively easy to come by, learning how to behave and how to carry yourself in order to progress are far more important at this stage.

Seeking out a mentor is vital at this point, too. Try to make a formal arrangement, if you can. Find a mentor network online, or ask your HR department. Otherwise, quietly study the behaviour of a peer in an informal way. Make your observations very discreetly but consistently, taking notes on how far more experienced people deal with different situations. Doing this will set you at a huge advantage over the Hare, who would probably do far less (if any at all) of this type of learning. Hares generally think they already know the best path and want to blaze their own trail, regardless of those who have been successful before them. The Tortoise looks to learn from everyone around them, drawing positively and negatively from all experiences. Did an overreaction produce a negative result? Did no reaction at all get a positive result? By constantly analysing a range of circumstances around you and seeing how they played out, you're regularly learning and progressing as a Tortoise, and arming yourself with the necessary tools to handle future situations. This is your on-the-job training. Taking the long, slow route is the very reason why the Tortoise is at an advantage. By observing in the background, then through direct personal experience, the Tortoise learns from mistakes and lessons while the Hare is busy pushing to get ahead at all costs.

My First Job

When I officially started working in my dream industry, I was based at a tennis academy run by a governing body. At the outset, I was fortunate enough to be asked to choose which academy I wanted to work at, and so I picked the one that had the edgiest and most experienced coaches of all. Even before I got there, I was warned to be 'ready for fireworks' and expect to feel uncomfortable. Boy, were they right! Day one: I arrived thinking I knew a thing or two. And I was going to let everyone there know it. At my very first team meeting, I made a few loose comments and was nailed. I was shocked. This had never happened to me before in a working environment. From that moment, I knew that to survive there I was going to have to put in some hard graft and do a lot of listening. Those coaches shaped me completely, blew away any arrogance or complacency I had and taught me the very meaning of substance and loyalty. They were ruthlessly hard and altruistically supportive at the same time. My first job taught me the importance of pushing yourself to work in environments that take you out of your comfort zone, with people who challenge you every day.

COMMUNICATING UPWARDS

When communicating at any stage of your career, always remember which way you're facing – upwards, downwards or laterally, peer to peer. As a Tortoise, when communicating upwards to management, you can bring to bear your patience, persistence, reliability and humility. Here are the most relevant things to consider when doing this:

1   Listening is far more important than talking at this point in your professional life.

2   Appear keen to listen, enthusiastic to learn.

3   Don't overcomplicate answers or use ten words where one will do.

4   Be honest if you don't know the answer to a question – bluffing will be sniffed out. Having the confidence to say 'I don't know' and expressing a desire to learn will actually be more impressive.

5   If you're asked to complete a task, ask a few relevant questions to be clear on it, then get on with it. Too many questions and you'll come across as either incompetent or unable to think for yourself.

6   Play the long game. You may be perceived as a threat by staff at middle-management level, who can potentially stifle your progress. This may be a reason for occasional hostility or a rejection of good ideas. The Tortoise approach is to accept this and continue working hard. Your views will be heard in time.

COMMUNICATING TO COLLEAGUES AND PEERS

Workplaces can be complicated in terms of hierarchy, especially when you're new and trying to work out who's who. Accept that you're going to make some mistakes with your colleagues. Form as many good bonds with these people as possible – it's highly likely you'll move through your career with this same peer group, and having a strong connection with them will open doors further down the line.

It's also key to seek advice from peers in similar roles, especially from those with expertise in specific or niche areas. As you technically have the most to learn at this stage in your career, you need to throw as much time, energy and resources as possible into learning how to communicate well. That said, even if it's informally to begin with, start presenting your work and ideas to groups, including senior staff. But don't overcomplicate it. A common mistake is attempting to appear more advanced in your methodologies than you really are. I recall presenting an entire annual training plan to the academy coaches, going into such ridiculous detail as reducing training volume by 1 per cent each week, while increasing training intensity by 1 per cent. Thinking back to the confused faces of my colleagues reading this plan and promptly putting it to one side, I bury my head in my hands in embarrassment. That piece of work took me hours and hours to produce, and it was nothing but completely overcomplicated rubbish.

WHAT WOULD A SELF-AWARE TORTOISE DO AMONG EXPERTS?

- 'Act your wage' and stick closely to your own field of expertise.

- Don't drift into others' specialist areas. If you say the wrong thing on such a topic, it may undermine your knowledge in your own. For example, in my case, as a strength and conditioning coach, throwing out opinions on tennis players and their results can very often be frowned upon. Still to this day, if I have a point to make in this regard, I will frame it by posing a question to a tennis coach rather than saying it as a statement.

- Say yes to any and every opportunity to develop that comes your way.

- Find mentorship, continue reading, take training courses, keep learning.

ENTRY-LEVEL PHASES

Even within the various stages of your career, there are different phases in each. Pre-entry could last years or a matter of months, depending on your age, life experience and motivation. However, for a Tortoise who is intent on building a solid foundation for the rest of their career with invaluable experience and learning, this level tends to occupy approximately a decade.

So let's take a look here at the phases of an entry role. While I cannot accurately put timelines to each of them, I am quite certain that they will all happen. It might also be worth examining other aspects of your life to see where else these three phases occur and how you might tackle them there.

Honeymoon Phase

While the name of this opening phase is usually associated with personal relationships, it certainly applies to job roles, too. This describes the early years, where there's an innocence and a freshness of approach. For the entry-level employee, this is where energy and excitement are at their highest. You combine a positive outlook with naivety to run head on into any problem, usually coming out the other side relatively unscathed, adding another learning experience to your portfolio.

The honeymoon phase is where the most mistakes occur, and are forgiven, for two reasons. Firstly, you're not expected to know any better; secondly, you're also new to those in your environment. There's a mutual politeness here. You'll find that most people show you a certain patience.

Consolidation Phase

With the honeymoon phase over, people now know what you are about. They've learned your strengths and weaknesses and have decided whether they like you and if your style of operating is for them or not.

One big change is that your ideas are less impactful. While there may be less energy around your input, the phrase 'familiarity breeds contempt' is certainly applicable here. Hence, it's common for people to experience a plateau in their feelings of effectiveness in this stage.

From a positive perspective, however, you're more trusted and are learning the ropes. You're also figuring out the direction you want to take, the people you find the most relatable and the subjects you're most passionate about.

I'm a firm believer in the specialization of skills. Once you've picked the general field you want to operate in, it's time to think about the specific area in which to develop expertise. The potential downside of a niche is that you could restrict your appeal to a broader market. I'm not suggesting that you don't have a grip on your field in general, just that you drill deeper with your knowledge of it to find a specific subject. The key to real success is finding a specialism which is relatively untapped, yet will be in huge demand now or in the future. Difficult, but far from impossible.

I knew I wanted to work in tennis from a young age. From there, I drilled down to become a strength and conditioning coach and form my niche. Others I know have become even more specialized in the field of strength and conditioning for tennis players, for example making themselves an authority on improving players' movement on the court. Some have gone a step further and become serve-and-volley movement experts. By doing this, you separate yourself from everyone else working in your industry. You also create a specific demand that may not even have existed before. Once you do this, word will spread and people will pay you more for your unique knowledge. They will fly you around the world to take seminars on your area of specialization. To me, this is a far more advantageous position than becoming a jack of all trades, master of none.

Challenge Phase

In the case of your career, the final entry phase determines whether you progress to promotion or leave the job to reinvent yourself elsewhere. Of course, your success in the first two stages has a strong influence on how the challenge phase will go. The reason for its name is that the chances of threats or challenges are at their highest here. These can come from a lack of energy, contempt for failures in earlier

Developing Your Niche

- Envision yourself as a world-renowned expert in a specific niche.

- Imagine being the expert speaker at conferences.

- Think about what kind of opportunities may open up to you if you made it. Even picture how much of an impact you could potentially make in your industry.

- What legacy do you want to leave? Is that a source of motivation for you?

- Make a step-by-step plan detailing how you intend to realize this dream.

- Note down the standards you must achieve to become truly world class and how you intend to set about upskilling.

- Seek out other people who have made it at this level and learn about them. How do they operate? What qualifications do they possess that you may not currently have? Can you spend time with them?

- Fully commit to your chosen path. Essentially, do anything and everything it takes to get there and don't stop until you do.

stages, the appointment of others in the same role who are in their honeymoon phase or even new management.

If you've started to develop your niche and are pursuing

a new and exciting direction, there will be high energy, enthusiasm and optimism around your contribution to the cause. If you haven't managed to specialize or put in extra work and thought into your direction, you may well be seen with cynicism by your superiors at this stage.

In personal relationships, you'd call this period the 'Seven-Year Itch', which suggests that happiness in marriages declines after such a time. Regardless, an honest assessment of current status is required. To rescue the situation, search hard for ideas to inject energy, passion and enthusiasm.

SUMMARIZING YOUR EXPERIENCE AT ENTRY LEVEL

There are no easy yards in a successful career. Entry level is where you take the most crap, do the dullest tasks and are given the least respect and responsibility. As I've said all along, this is fine, it's normal and every Tortoise goes through it.

The Tortoise values we explored in Chapter Three are as important as ever in this period of your professional life. Being humble with a low ego, being persistent and playing the long game with consistent high effort and patience are key. You will have your head down enough to avoid attracting negativity, but your relentless hard work and intelligent approach will get you noticed, as you become increasingly competent and experienced.

At entry level, you'll also be meeting the people who will be pivotal to you as you progress in your career. In fact, I shared one of my very first gym instructor jobs with an excellent colleague who I now work with in elite-level tennis. I've known many of the strength and conditioning coaches whom I work with today for over a decade and more, and consider them to be close friends.

Every single one of the Tortoise attributes got me through these first years at the academy. I used them instinctively to navigate my way through this time. I can't ever imagine skipping this entry step and working with professional players immediately. I would've been completely out of my depth. I wouldn't have been able to cope with the stress or the pressure, I wouldn't have built the substance or character to face these big personalities, and I simply would not have backed myself.

The Tortoise characteristics you have and the Tortoise values you develop will get you through this first career stage and make you ready to dominate the next, so roll up your sleeves and be an energizer!

NOW YOU DO IT

My description of this phase is unashamedly based on extensive personal experience. There's also some advice, which, if you're currently at this point in your professional life, you won't feel much like taking – but trust me on this: it's essential.

- First and foremost, you must continue to commit totally and utterly to your chosen path.

- Be the first to arrive and the last to leave. Ensure that being around you is a positive experience for people and doesn't require a great deal of their energy.

- As you have very little experience or credibility at this level, how you conduct yourself is vital; endear yourself to senior colleagues, don't repel them.

- Senior staff may be dismissive of you. Accept this and know that they too had to go through this stage (maybe worse, maybe longer) to get to their current position.

- Only involve yourself in debates if you are 100 per cent certain that you're factually correct. As Abraham Lincoln quite wisely stated, 'Better to say nothing and be thought a fool than to open your mouth and remove all doubt.'

- You will have strong opinions but almost no experience with which to back them up. Better to keep them to yourself. Only express them to your peers or mention to senior staff in private.

- As high energy, passion and enthusiasm are your strengths, say yes to everything asked of you and do it well.

- Excel at the menial jobs, too – believe it or not, you'll build trust and respect by doing this. It's a rite of passage.

Your next step is the level of middle management, where you become the expert with newbies below you and influencers above. You now have inexperienced people who look up to you. You've been there and can empathize. Yet there's still plenty to learn and people you need to answer to.

MIDDLE MANAGEMENT (10–20 YEARS)

As the facilitator of upper-level management policy, your role here is pivotal. You have established respect with those new to the industry and are a mentor or manager to them, as well as being entrusted by senior management to represent their aspirations, values and goals to the rest of the company. Being the fulcrum between these two points of balance requires great skill, especially to maintain respect from both sides.

The first thing to remember when starting a role in middle management is the reason why you've been appointed in the first place. What are the skills and experiences that have got you here? You have been employed for what you know, not what you don't know. You have been given this position for who you are, not who you aren't.

MAKING AN OPENING STATEMENT

In April 2010, the Great Britain Davis Cup team was facing relegation to the bottom tier of world tennis when the Lawn Tennis Association appointed Leon Smith as captain. I was fortunate enough to be asked to join the team as the strength and conditioning coach. It was in the very first staff team meeting that Leon set out his vision for the future with the following vision statement: 'A well-prepared team on a journey back to the World Group' (the top tier of international men's team tennis).

Leon then went on to expand on the team's mission with the following goals:

- **Prepared** – we were going to prepare better than any other team, both in how we treated our own players and how we scouted the opposition.

- **Team** – we were going to behave and act like a great team, creating an unrivalled team spirit.

- **Journey** – we recognized that, while things can't happen overnight, we had a plan and needed time to develop our processes and build confidence.

I was so impressed with several things in this meeting. First, the clarity of the vision statement. It was simple, yet encapsulated so much about the work and culture we were about to put in place. It was also ambitious, but achievable. The team was languishing in the lower echelons of world tennis, but had the talent and the resources to get right back to the very top.

Hearing this confidence from the leader was powerful in that moment. And finally, it was well defined in the mission. There could be no ambiguity in what Leon was asking, both of the staff and of the players. To me, though, by far the most impressive aspect of that meeting was how Leon delivered this message. He had a clear vision and a complete conviction that it would happen. Every single team member left that room feeling like they were a valued part of something special and that we were all heading in the same direction together. It was one of the best examples of leadership that I had witnessed in my career so far.

Five years later, Great Britain won the Davis Cup by beating USA, France, Australia and, eventually, Belgium in the final. The team had gone on an almost vertical trajectory, gaining two group promotions and beating every other Grand Slam nation en route to winning the competition. The team spirit was the same from the very first relegation play-off tie to the final, and it continues to this day.

At a dinner held on the evening of the title win, I asked Leon if I could give a speech. It was addressed to our team, though the Belgian team among others was also in the room.

I wanted to make the point that, as impressive as Great Britain's victory had been, it had come as no surprise to me. It certainly wasn't intended to sound arrogant or disrespectful to the opposition, but to simply say that the right process and culture had been in place for five years and that the team had been preparing properly for such a moment for a long time. Both Leon and the players deserved the credit they got, for a job well done and a memory that none of us will forget.

Starting a role where you've become responsible for other people often brings with it a level of fear and trepidation. The very best way to deal with any fear is to be prepared for it. Following on from the example of Leon Smith, the next section has an exercise to help you with that.

CREATING YOUR VISION STATEMENT

This exercise lays out your vision, intention and affirmations about yourself. Set it all out prior to your first day in your management position. In simple terms, think about: what you want to achieve so you're viewed as an overwhelming success; what this actually looks like; and, last but not least, how you want to 'be' in achieving it.

1   **Take the pressure off.** Be kind to yourself in terms of your expectations of immediate success. You will have an impact in time. You're new to this position – it may even be your very first management position. So, be aware that it's likely to take you several years (if not a decade) to become a master of this stage. Only a Hare would step into this position with expectations of overnight success. Make allowances for learning and making mistakes along the way.

2   **Write out your vision and mission statement.** What
    do you want this department to achieve? Brainstorm
    the kind of words that you want people to associate
    with your team and the work. Think about what you
    want everyone to establish, the reputation they'll have
    to live and die by in order to achieve the outcome. And
    then put all this into a couple of sentences that makes
    sense.

3   **State who you are.** Write out a statement about who
    you are. What are your strengths? How do others
    see you as a positive role model and leader already?
    What examples of success have you had in managing
    situations to date? What did upper management or
    key clients see in you to give you this role? Recall
    their positive feedback statements. Then write out
    a statement about how you want to be, including as
    many words as possible that capture your Tortoise
    characteristics and values.

4   **Set out your stages for achieving the vision.** What
    will have to be in place? What phases will your
    team need to go through? What problems must be
    overcome? Take note of potential threats and issues
    that could arise, as well as fears that the team may
    have. You don't need to discuss these publicly, but be
    prepared for them if they are brought to you.

5   **Share your vision statement with the team on
    day one of your new role.** You can do this exercise
    together, using your team's words as well as your own.
    Even though these techniques are fairly commonly
    understood management strategies, my emphasis

here is on the soft skills around the delivery of these strategies. It's not the strategy so much as *how* you deliver it to your team that makes the difference. You must believe in the vision statement more than anyone else in the room. You must communicate this with absolute clarity and an intensity of purpose that make it very hard to take issue with. Now is the time for the Tortoise characteristic of passion to come to the forefront. Be excited about it. Bring the vision to life by setting out the possibilities that could be realized for everyone as a collective, if they work together to achieve them. With doubters, or those who question the vision, be firm but not overly confrontational. In this moment, it's important for your team to see that you have the courage of your convictions. They should leave the room energized, valued, clear and convinced they are going to be a part of something that's not only correct, but worthwhile and special.

6 **At all times, be strong.** How does this look? Positive, not pessimistic. Energized, not flat. Firm, but fair. Assertive, not aggressive. Clear, not ambiguous. Unshakeable, not flappable. Consistent, not erratic. Reactive if required, but primarily sticking to your plan.

COMMUNICATING UPWARDS TO THE SENIOR TEAM

Your level of accountability is high, both above and below you on the corporate chain. The first thing you have to tell yourself is that you're in your position on merit, so hold your own and don't fawn or be a 'Yes' person. Show strength in your views without being argumentative. Understand from the beginning that having a record of what has been

My First Leadership Roles

My first leadership experience was managing a gym for a UK chain of health clubs. In retrospect, I was out of my depth. The balance I found the trickiest to reach was the desire to be popular with the team of gym instructors, personal trainers and aerobics teachers, while maintaining a mutually respectful distance. As a result, I feared conflict and, in most cases, wasn't strong enough. That said, in a very short space of time I did learn a great deal about the business side of the health and fitness industry, and it prepared me for my next role as National Lead for Strength and Conditioning within the Lawn Tennis Association. As I'd worked for the company and in tennis for such a long time, by the time I got this leadership role I'd already established a reasonable amount of respect with my co-workers, in my own Tortoise-like way. Although I still had more lessons to learn on the people management side of the role, I had made significant improvements there and felt effective. By this stage, I was travelling on the tennis tour for fifteen to twenty weeks of the year, so my biggest issue was managing remotely. When you're physically not where the players are, things can often go unnoticed and issues unreported for weeks. So, as a manager, I learned that over-communication and having your finger on the pulse in all situations are vital. By the time I came to lead the support team for Andy Murray, I was working at a level whereby each individual team member was an industry leader in their own right. When managing such people, I came to recognize what I could change and have an impact on. Just as importantly, I also began to accept what I simply could not change.

communicated in meetings, corridor conversations and performance reviews is vitally important.

1 Communicate with senior managers on a formal basis, unless they take it to an informal level.

2 Don't be the one to initiate personal conversations with them.

3 Big decisions will be made by you and for you, so make it a priority to have a clear record of reasoning and evidence of what has been said for you to recall at a later date.

4 Get as much in writing as possible.

COMMUNICATING TO FELLOW MANAGERS

You're a middle manager, but never forget you're a Tortoise. Use the watch-and-learn tactics you practised at entry level – some managers will be doing a great job and some will be making clear mistakes. Make a note of both and see how they apply to your practice.

Other than one or two close friends, keep relations on the more formal side in this role. Do not readily admit weakness, failures or internal problems with your team – it's not ideal to have gossip around these issues.

COMMUNICATING TO YOUR TEAM

Whatever the size of your team, it's important to balance being a respected leader with invoking a positive, supportive working environment. Be someone whom your team feels that they can talk to and trust, but who also has the best interests of the company and the mission at heart.

You ought to find yourself doing a lot of listening – your job isn't just to tell everyone what to do. The people reporting to you will want to feel like they are respected and empowered. They will be looking to you to have their ideas and feelings validated.

Meetings, meetings. Always finish them with clear action points and start the next one with a progress report. Follow up quickly on what is agreed in these meetings. Be consistent, too – never promise your team something unless you know for a fact you can deliver it. Always have your vision statement in the front of your mind to refer to when you have decisions to make.

Does it Make the Boat Go Faster?

In 1998, the Great Britain Men's Rowing Eight team was struggling to make the finals of major competitions, so they decided to fundamentally question everything about their approach. The key question they asked themselves about every decision was 'Does it make the boat go faster?' If any action plan or decision was made which didn't affect their performance in the boat, they decided to stop doing it and concentrate only on important factors. This resulted in them winning the gold medal two years later at the Sydney 2000 Olympic Games. Therefore, as the leader of your team, you must ask this about every discussion and idea put forward – 'Does it make the boat go faster?' 'Does it bring us closer to achieving our mission?' If it doesn't, then don't waste time doing it, even if it seems like a good idea.

PHASES WITHIN STAGES

As with entry level, the middle-management stage has three phases to it – honeymoon, consolidation and challenge. Let's look at these again in this new context.

Honeymoon Phase

This stage is where your vision statement exercise comes into play. Your ability to have an immediate impact will never be greater than here. Your team's enthusiasm to hear your message is also never likely to be greater than at this point. Hopefully, upper management will also have the most enthusiasm for your ideas now. Your ability to ask for a budget and to make things happen is also at its highest. Make sure you use all these factors to give yourself the best possible start in the role.

While part one of the vision statement exercise makes allowances for mistakes in this new job, you cannot afford to be reckless here. You are the team's manager. Faith will be lost both above and below if too many errors occur as time progresses. So, be mindful in times where you've made one inevitable mistake not to immediately follow this up with another.

This phase reminds me of the time I was flying abroad on my own to a training camp in 2016. I was the last to get on the plane, and as I approached my seat I saw that the one next to me was occupied by a renowned football manager in the English Premier League. Remembering my less-is-more strategy, I simply politely said hello and left him to his own devices. With approximately an hour left of the flight, he engaged in conversation with me and we began exchanging anecdotes about our lives in sport as well as some mutual contacts we had. He was incredibly smart, ambitious, driven and energized, all of the virtues that I would hope to one day embody. One piece of advice he passed on to me had been given to him by another world-famous football manager: 'Plan for the wedding and also plan for the funeral.'

The cut-throat nature of the job in elite-level football means managers are not expected to stay in their roles for a long period of time. Therefore, they must employ the strategy of playing two or three moves ahead, as we looked at previously in the Tortoise value of perspective. This manager's advice was to use the Honeymoon stage not only to negotiate good terms for himself at the start, but also to take the opportunity, when energy and positivity around him was high, to put in place a favourable exit strategy for the time when, inevitably, things were not as good.

The importance of having this plan already in place at the beginning struck me as genius. Not to be negotiating my personal severance pay in any of my jobs, but to be implementing strategies at the start of a job as contingencies for problems further down the track. You know there'll be Consolidation and Challenge phases ahead. So, while the entry-level worker must develop a niche to help them through these stages, what should the middle manager do?

Consolidation Phase

The emphasis here is about making sure that you and your team are working towards the vision set out in your opening statement. Clearly, now you've left the honeymoon phase, everyone will be well versed but also less likely to be excited about this plan. Now, it's your role as leader to avoid this becoming a trend.

Performing a robust audit of your plan so far is particularly important in the consolidation phase. For this, ask some very honest questions about the successes and failures to date. Which team members are delivering their aspect of the plan well and identifying areas for improvement? It's your job to shake things up and provide a stimulus for renewed enthusiasm. This could be by opening up the floor to the team for feedback, introducing a competitive element to delivery by incentivizing people or even making changes to personnel.

It can be all too easy to write a plan at the beginning of a project, only to divert away from it once some of the roadblocks appear. So, going back to your original intentions and revisiting the values and behaviours you initially set out can be very powerful. It reminds everyone of the cornerstones of this project and ought to get all, including yourself, back on the same page.

Avoid changing your original statements as you go along. The clarity of vision and passion you had at the start of the role is forever powerful. Before you get bogged down in micro-managing issues of the politics of the job, you had a dream for it. You must always bring yourself back to that vision and those virtues, and ask yourself 'How true am I being to the mission statement and to myself?' Not being true to yourself can be catastrophic. Those above and below you could lose faith in your ability to deliver. The next plan you make will be met with less enthusiasm at best, lip service at worst. Referring back to the plan in times of pressure not only allows for confidence in it to grow, but it also shows everyone that you believe in it as much as you ever did. If you make major deviations from your plan as soon as problems arise, all faith in it and you will be gone.

Challenge Phase

Success in this final phase of your middle-management job largely depends on how successful the previous stages have been. Threats for the middle manager come in the guise of structural change or fresh blood being brought in via management audits or internal promotion. It's important not to take these threats personally – they're perfectly normal once you reach this level of your career. That's not to say they aren't stressful, because people usually have a lot more to lose once they're at this stage, maybe a large mortgage to pay for and a family to support.

With the stakes at their highest and the pressure from threats ever present by this challenge phase, many managers start to make decisions and exhibit behaviours purely based on keeping their job. Tempting though this is, it's actually the last thing you should be doing as a Tortoise.

Regardless of outcome, the following three steps are the correct way to conduct yourself in the difficult challenge phase. Managers who have been in the job many years will see several of these challenges come and go. If you survive change, you will likely return to consolidation or even honeymoon phases if you have a new team or new senior management. You may of course get promotion. If you've conducted yourself well throughout, there will be many others who have not. And that's exactly how the Tortoise wins the race – not panicking, but sticking to the plan and its values.

LISTEN TO YOUR INNER TORTOISE

Now is the time to refer back to steps 1–6 of the vision statement.

- **Take pressure off yourself.** Use kind and positive language when thinking about how you've performed in the role and remember that pressure is perfectly normal for people in your position. If you've put everything you could into the job, then that's all you could ask of yourself and all that those above could expect of you. You were given that job for the knowledge and skills you have, not for those you lacked. So, be proud of your efforts. Whatever happens, others will see the same qualities in you.

- **Stick to your plan.** Only deviate if you've been given a clear steer from senior management that says you must.

- **Be the Tortoise.** Refer back to the values, positive statements and affirmations you wrote at the very beginning of this job. Make additional notes of the successes you've enjoyed. Write these down with Hare-like overconfidence for once. Every manager in the world has been through this. Are you going to crumble and fade, becoming a sycophant to upper management? Or, will you show fortitude, dig your heels in, redouble your efforts and fight harder? Remember the power of holding your position. There's great strength and tactical advantage in not reacting, or seeking a reaction, but in simply continuing with your work, showing a positive attitude and watching how things play out. Those are the leadership qualities that got you the job in the first place.

SUMMARIZING YOUR MIDDLE-MANAGEMENT EXPERIENCE

Middle management is one of the most rewarding but challenging phases of your career. You have established respect within the industry and are able to implement your ideas and the things you've learned with your own team of people. With that comes responsibility from above, as well as a duty of care below. Keeping both happy is a difficult task, which will draw upon all of your resources and skills of communication.

Your peers are other managers, too. In many ways, you'll also be seeing this group as competitors. While I'm not suggesting you spend much time fearing structural change, be aware that middle management can be the part of the organization to take a hit or be streamlined. Knowing this, you'll be working hard to become one of the more competent and confident managers in the group.

- The first temptation is to dramatically change your behaviour, the way you speak to others and your conduct in general; this is a mistake, especially if you've been promoted from within and are now managing your former peers.

- Making small adjustments may need to happen, but this must be over a long period of time.

- Assess your current relationships with former peers and think about where you'd like these relationships to be in a few months' time; refer back to your working relationships exercise (see page 168).

- Don't pretend to be an expert in all things. You may now oversee people with entirely different hard skill sets to your own, with even better skills than you have in your own niche. This is absolutely fine and a perfectly normal position to be in. Having some fears about this is also reasonable.

- Prepare for conversations with the people you're overseeing by thinking about which skills you have that could be of use to them; time management, people skills, connections and contacts all may come in useful.

- Avoid the temptation to enforce your knowledge and abilities on your most competent people; think about holding your position, waiting for issues to arise or for them to come to you with a problem and then offer your skills and advice.

- Involve your team in creating a mission statement. Working on words associated with behaviours and values together as a team can be a very effective way of gaining buy-in and commitment.

- Avoid putting your cards on the table about the team's performance, just focus primarily on your plan and processes within your team and let everything else take care of itself.

Up, down and sideways, the overriding message is to know who you are, recognize the skills you've been rewarded for and, finally, to have a plan and stick to it through thick and thin. Once again, be the Tortoise and hold your position.

OPTIMIZING YOUR TORTOISE STRENGTHS

- You'll need your Tortoise strengths to work for you at each and every stage of your career: from pre-entry to entry level; then from middle-management roles to upper management.

- At each career stage, you'll be using your Tortoise values to work out how to communicate upwards to senior management, sideways to your peers and downwards to your team.

- When you enter a new career stage, you'll find your strengths tested in the honeymoon phase and can expect to pass through two other stages over the course of the role – consolidation and challenge.

- The pre-entry stage calls for your positive energy and enthusiasm as you knock on as many doors as possible and refuse to take no for an answer.

- The entry-level stage is your first paid role, in which you could spend anything up to ten years honing the Tortoise values of patience and persistence, as you watch, listen and learn.

- You could have several middle-management roles and each one will depend on how well you set out your opening statement and carry the team with you through the different phases of your position.

7

WINNING FRIENDS
THE TORTOISE WAY

One of the major challenges facing aspirational people is
how to get their ideas and concepts across to those who
have the authority or financial power to implement them.
Imagine you're working for a large organization and have a
new idea or innovation to present to the hierarchy. Or, perhaps
you're an entrepreneur presenting to potential investors. You
might actually be a coach sharing a new concept or drill with
your peers. You could even be a student showing a new theory
to your professor. The challenge is the same and its outcome
depends on several things:

- the quality of the idea itself.

- how much it challenges existing behaviours and
  beliefs.

- how practical it is to implement.

- the timing, depending on the political or financial
  climate within the organization.

For me, there's also no getting away from another vitally
important factor: the relative level of industry experience of
the person presenting the idea to their audience.

APPRECIATE YOUR PROBLEM

An idea can tick several or all of the boxes above, but often it's not enough. In our working lives, certain realities exist that we may not like but have to contend with nonetheless. One of these is that experience often leads to status, and status leads to power.

Hares would challenge this, but even they are forced to fit in with structures of lineage in business and even society. Hares are typically very passionate about their ideas and tend to adopt a tunnel-vision approach, not quite understanding why anyone would hold an opposing view. In an attempt to have their idea become a reality at any cost, they will seek out any stakeholders that agree with it and often devalue those who don't support it. It can be an unpopular approach for people around them, but they don't care. That said, it can also be impactful and quicker than the Tortoise approach of taking other people's positions and perspectives into account.

My point here is that, before going in to sell a concept, you must have an appreciation of your position. It will have an impact on your likelihood of success. Both your expectations and your preparation should be aligned prior to engaging. Setting realistic expectations in this scenario is not an attempt to discourage or demotivate, far from it. Often in my career, especially early on, I would feel very frustrated when my ideas were not embraced. I felt disrespected or patronized, as though I wasn't being heard. Again, the reality was that I was simply surrounded by those with more experience, who had often either tried such concepts before and knew they didn't or wouldn't work, or already had established successful methods for the same problem. Alternatively, they might have welcomed a good new idea. Either way, that shouldn't have influenced how I felt about myself. That's easy to say now. Hopefully, after gaining an appreciation of this process, you will feel the same, too!

Let me introduce you now to something that I think will help you to work through the dilemmas and opportunities that come with courting influence and getting people at all levels of an organization to buy in to your ideas.

THE TORTOISE BUY-IN MATRIX

Based on the experience I've had through different stages of my career, I have created the buy-in matrix in this chapter to help you to think about who you need to talk to and influence when promoting your ideas. You might be surprised to learn that this isn't always upper management. More often than not, it's about getting the people who work at your level or in your team to accept your idea and make it happen. Sometimes, ideas that are signed off by upper management turn out to be unworkable lower down because they aren't in touch with the reality of implementation at those levels. It's not just about getting sign-off, but working on the likelihood of successful implementation, too. That's what we really mean by 'buy-in' in any organization.

The buy-in matrix breaks experience levels down into three simple stages previously mentioned in the book: 0–10 years entry level/newbie; 10–20 years middle management/expert; and 20+ years upper management or influencer.

Running down the side of the matrix is the experience level of the presenter of the idea. Running along the top is the audience they are attempting to convince. The shading gradation represents the presenter's chances of buy-in.

THE BUY-IN MATRIX

	AUDIENCE		
	Entry level/ newbie 0–10 years	Middle management/ expert 10–20 years	Upper management/ influencer 20+ years
PRESENTER Entry level/ newbie 0–10 years	Medium chance of buy-in	Low chance of buy-in	Low chance of buy-in
Middle mgmt/ expert 10–20 years	High chance of buy-in	Medium chance of buy-in	Low chance of buy-in
Upper mgmt/ influencer 20+ years	High chance of buy-in	High chance of buy-in	Low chance of buy-in

High chance of buy-in	Medium chance of buy-in	Low chance of buy-in

WINNING PEOPLE OVER WHEN YOU'RE AT ENTRY LEVEL

When you're an entry-level newbie, your colleagues at the same level are also fairly inexperienced and limited in knowledge. Influencing them isn't impossible, but nor is success guaranteed. So, be prepared for a medium chance of buy-in with your ideas.

Moving on to the likelihood of middle management embracing your concept, however, you can expect a low level of success. For this idea to win them over, irrefutable evidence is required and it must be an excellent idea through and through. In most cases, it should also cause minimal disruption to the modus operandi and be very easy to implement.

Finally, when an entry-level employee gets the chance to present to upper management, unsurprisingly it has the most unlikely chance of success on the matrix. The only possible opportunities arise if the influencer seeks an opinion on a specific issue with which they have less experience, such as a new technology in the industry. Or, if the newbie asks questions in such a way as to make the influencer believe it was their idea.

GETTING BUY-IN WHEN YOU'RE AT MIDDLE-MANAGEMENT LEVEL

An expert middle manager will clearly have influence over their newbie colleagues. While little or no evidence or justification is required here, there is a role to educate on the reasons for the decision. Even though the chances of buy-in and consequent implementation are high, the entry-level audience may also have their own views on how to do things here.

At the middle manager's peer level, there's a high potential for egos to clash. Based on their own agenda, both parties will feel like they know the right decision. At this stage, informal standing within the organization or having a specific level of expertise around the subject is likely to win through. In this situation, there's only a moderate chance of buy-in.

When presenting a concept to influencers, there is again a reasonable chance of buy-in for middle managers. Much depends on the following factors:

→ **Relationship** between the two parties. People tend to feel that this isn't relevant, but people liking each other at work will have an influence on buy-in, especially here.

→ **Trust.** Does the 'expert' have a track record of successful ideas?

→ **Evidence.** This is important with any idea in this situation.

Rightly so, the middle manager can expect a moderate-to-good chance of their concepts being adopted across the board.

AGREEMENT AND IMPLEMENTATION AT UPPER-MANAGEMENT LEVEL

Clearly, upper management should expect buy-in. Never more so than when addressing entry-level workers. This is, of course, the most autocratic scenario. Again, middle managers are likely to buy in, too. The influencer will be interested in the expert's feedback, especially around how the organization will be affected, as the middle manager may have a better feel for this at the coal face.

Last, but not least, when influencers combine, this *should* be the purest form of decision-making. Both have a very good understanding of their field and objectivity ought to dominate the discussion – in theory. However, these people tend to have the largest egos, so there's potentially the least chance of compromise. That said, as with all the peer-to-peer interactions on the matrix, a moderate chance of success applies.

MY GOAL FOR YOU

In this chapter, you'll have recognized many of the real situations that you face in the workplace, as well as in your personal life. You'll be thinking about how so much of what we've looked at applies to everybody, whether Hare or Tortoise. In which case, how can you, a Tortoise, outwit the more outwardly confident and flamboyant Hare?

If we think back to the skills drills in Chapter Five, we know that accessing the Tortoise toolkit of skills and becoming adept at handling these situations will not only greatly improve your chances of succeeding in your career, but also raise your confidence levels and other people's perception of you.

The overriding factor in almost every scenario is to plan for it. Ask yourself these questions:

- 'How do I want to be in this situation?'

- 'How would I like others to see me handle this?'

- 'What approach is not only going to give me the best chance of success, but a mutually beneficial outcome, where both parties feel good at the end?'

We know that Hares simply do not think like this. Self-aware or not, they just expect to win through. We've also seen how this scenario often plays out. Of course, the reality is that by just reading this chapter, you will improve very little. Soft skills are just that – skills. And any world-class operator in their field will practise their skills to a level that most others would not. They arrive early and stay late to practise more often. Even when they go home, they are still practising. The way of the Tortoise is not simply to rely on talents, but to show consistent hard work, be fully committed and to never be outworked by anyone. By following this process often enough, those skills improve to a level where they become automatic. Where you develop the power to hold your position, reacting appropriately and only when required. Where you become a Tortoise who is totally prepared for the rigours of the world, equipped to handle any scenario. *This* is my goal for you.

GET READY FOR BOOT CAMP

Your first step in this book was simply to read. The easy part. Your second is to go out and put into action all that you've read! The best way to begin is to go through what we call in the strength and conditioning field a 'shock micro-cycle', otherwise known as a boot camp. This is where your body spends a week performing exercises that it's not used to and training at a volume and intensity it's not used to. All with the goal of shocking it into change.

We're about to perform the same boot camp intervention with your mindset. You're going to spend a week practising every skill in this book. Learning, adapting, making mistakes and learning again.

The Tortoise Boot Camp exercises in the following pages fall into three categories. Most develop soft skills for situations you can plan for and then put that plan into action immediately. Other exercises are ongoing, in that you won't see immediate change. You'll still have to make a plan for them, but be more patient in seeing the results; for example, becoming a better team player.

The final category is purely situational. Managing change, dealing with a high-achieving individual and reactive conflict are the three subjects that fit this mould. Being au fait with the strategy in these scenarios is the most important aspect of preparation, but you can't seek these scenarios out. They will just happen when they happen, so be ready.

There is some good news here. This is the way of the *Tortoise*, not the way of the Shaolin monk. The challenges you face in boot camp will take you out of your comfort zone, but not so that you feel overawed by them. Your work colleagues should not think that you've become an entirely different person overnight ... and no, you will not need to uproot trees with your bare hands or break bricks on your head. However, the goal is still to change your behaviours over time and potentially become a much more rounded practitioner and person. Therefore, the Tortoise Boot Camp is something you can easily commit to doing. And the more often you repeat this week of exercises, the better Tortoise you will become.

Something else you should notice is that some of the exercises will come more naturally to you than others. At the end of the week, therefore, it's important to take note of which ones you found the most challenging and repeat them as often as you can. We only like to practise what we're good at, but no lasting change happens in the comfort zone. Show patience and fortitude – face these issues again and again until you overcome them.

In preparation for the Tortoise Boot Camp, you must adopt the right mindset and remind yourself of who you are and how you want to be. If you've not already done this, it is now time to take the Tortoise Test. Identify your strengths and the areas that you need to work on. Have these in mind when you start the boot camp. This is your Tortoise identity and it's a great time to have an attitude reset to prepare you for giving the best effort you possibly can. You're a Tortoise. You can do this.

YOU AND YOUR POWER OF INFLUENCE

- No matter what your position or career stage, you have to regularly influence others at all levels, so it's worthwhile understanding and therefore maximizing your chances of success.

- The Buy-in Matrix helps you to think about what you're presenting and to whom, taking into account the likelihood of getting others to sign up to your ideas and, just as importantly, to implement them.

- At such times, you'll come up against Hares and you'll need to remind yourself of all your Tortoise characteristics, values and strengths.

- As a Tortoise, you have your own very different ways of influencing people and gaining buy-in, but only constant practice and resetting yourself will help you to win in the end.

Tortoise
Boot Camp

The point of any boot camp is the shock of the effort you're required to make, usually over a short space of time. For a Tortoise, this might sound counterintuitive. But I wouldn't be suggesting it if I didn't know it worked.

Firstly, let's define what I mean by micro-cycle. It is commonly used in the world of athletic development to demarcate the shortest cycle, or period of training, which is designed to achieve a specific outcome. This is usually a week-long in duration.

A shock micro-cycle takes things a little further. It represents a sharp increase in training load, usually higher than the athlete has previously experienced. This kind of micro-cycle is designed to push you to your limits in order to stimulate adaptation and reach higher performance levels – in other words, a really tough week to get some fast gains!

So, fast gains are not something that a Tortoise is interested in because they are usually not sustainable. This is true and this is why shock micro-cycles are used sparingly when training athletes because they are not appropriate for long-term use and will burn athletes out. But, they are a great way to really kick-start some momentum and that's how I want you to use this week – to get you started on the road to true lasting change.

Here comes the commitment question: can you add Tortoise Boot Camp into an upcoming week of your life in the very near future? Perhaps you could think about taking a few days off to complete it, although realistically you might not have the spare holiday time to devote to career-changing activities – perhaps you can simply find extra time in your working week. Or you could follow actor Mark Wahlberg's example and wake up early to complete the morning task, then wait until 5 p.m. to complete the afternoon task. In many senses, being around your workmates while working on these soft skills means you can put them into immediate action. Perhaps you can do some of these activities as you commute to and from work. Alternatively, there's always your lunch break.

The great thing about all of the exercises is that every single minute you spend thinking of your answers to the questions they pose, every letter that you write down and reflect on, and even the smallest task you undertake, is a step in the right direction of being happier and more successful. There is absolutely no downside. Even if you come up with the wrong answers at first, at least you will know what doesn't work and what you don't want.

The reality is that, if you're currently thinking of reasons why you just don't have the time to commit to Tortoise Boot Camp, how much of a better, improved Tortoise are you really committed to becoming? This next step may be make or break for you in your journey to becoming a successful Tortoise. You've come this far, so let's push extra hard in these final stages.

Over the page is a sample week of Tortoise Boot Camp, but of course you can substitute different exercises into this template depending on what works for you. After the Boot Camp schedule, I'll link in the exercises to the appropriate pages in the book.

	MONDAY	TUESDAY	WEDNESDAY
AM	**A new dawn** Career Stage Exercise	**Future planning** Future Brainstorming Exercise	**Pressure** Internal Dialogue Exercise
PM	Communication Exercise	Successful Individual Case Study Exercise	Pressure Visualization Exercise

	THURSDAY	FRIDAY	SATURDAY	SUNDAY
AM	**People skills** Interpersonal Relationships Scaling Exercise	**Outcomes** Success Visualization Exercise	**Planning for ongoing skills** Tortoise Team Player Drill	**Planning continued** Success Snowball Exercise
PM	Empathy Exercise	Failure Visualization Exercise	Taking Care of Family/Loved Ones Drill	Buy-in Matrix

DAY 1 – MONDAY

Change starts now on Monday morning with a major project at your current career stage:

Pre-Entry – Foot in the Door Exercise (page 187)

Entry – Develop Your Niche Exercise (page 197)

Middle Management – Opening Statement Exercise (page 203)

Your key career stage exercise will be the one that sets the tone and gives you a vision and an action plan of who and what you want to be in the medium term. So, make it ambitious.

I expect that a project of this magnitude could take longer than a morning to plan and execute. Don't worry if you don't have this completely finished. There will be other tasks in the week that you will get through quickly, allowing you to go back and work on this one.

Day one is also a great time to think about the most important soft skill of them all: communication (see page 122). Thinking about the quantity and quality of how you interact and implementing an exercise to improve communication will give you a good start to the week.

DAY 2 – TUESDAY

We turn now to the future. With your plan and vision from day one clear in your mind, I want you to work through all of the possible connotations of your immediate future, as well as looking at someone who has achieved greatness over their career path. This will prepare and inspire you for the journey ahead.

Future Brainstorming Exercise (page 150)

Successful Individual Case Study Exercise (page 175)

DAY 3 – WEDNESDAY

Any journey worth taking will test you with many bumps in the road. Day three is when you start preparing for these bumps. Looking at how you deal with pressure will be an important step in steeling yourself when the inevitable comes.

Internal Dialogue Exercise (page 138)

Pressure Visualization Exercise (page 137)

DAY 4 – THURSDAY

On day four, we return to the subject of people and how you interact with them. This would be an opportune moment to revisit your communication exercise and look at your progress here, as well as assessing your relationships with those around you.

Interpersonal Relationships Scaling Exercise (page 168)

Empathy Exercise (page 116)

DAY 5 – FRIDAY

Towards the end of the week, on day five, I want you to visualize the potential outcomes that you hope to achieve. Visualization is such a powerful tool and the more you immerse yourself into these experiences, bring them to life and make them real to you, the more effective they will be. Ask yourself:

'How do I want these experiences to look?'

'How do I want them to sound?'

'How do I want them to feel?'

As with every soft skill, preparation allows you to be on the front foot straight away and thank yourself further down the track.

Success Visualization Exercise (page 146)

Failure Visualization Exercise (page 143)

DAY 6 – SATURDAY

On day six, even though it's the weekend, it's time to start making plans for your longer-term projects. Of course, none of the tasks are a one-off event, but you will realize the results more slowly.

Tortoise Team Player Drill (page 128)

Taking Care of Family/Loved Ones Drill (page 179)

DAY 7 – SUNDAY

Thinking about how you will become a better teammate, how you intend to look after your family and friends – these are such beneficial tasks. And in finishing the week, you'll be looking at all the little decisions you can make to start building successful momentum, as well as planning how you will get others around you to buy in to your ideas. This should give you confidence and inspiration.

Success Snowball Exercise (page 147)

Buy-in Matrix (page 219)

Like the success snowball exercise, the cumulative effect of putting a week aside to work on you and how you want to develop yourself will start you on a course that you never thought possible. You'll be facing questions about who you are, what you want to be, how you want to be and what all that actually looks like.

Don't rush the tasks and don't make promises to yourself that you can't keep. Be a Tortoise and take your time. Getting it right is far more important than getting it finished. If you hit a roadblock, walk away from that task for twenty minutes and do something else, then roll up your sleeves and attack it again. There's nothing in there that you aren't capable of doing.

CONCLUSION: ALL THINGS COME TO THOSE WHO WAIT

Anyone who has ever changed the course of their life has done so by using a huge amount of emotional strength. You see a photo of yourself you don't like, so you work to get fit. You get a health scare and decide you're going to live more in the now, enjoy life while you can. A negative comment from someone about your intelligence and you set off on a training course to show them who you really are. Minor or major, these events jolt you into saying to yourself, 'I'm not going to continue along the same path anymore. If I want to find happiness, I have to do something different.'

You're a Tortoise. Now, you know so much more about what that means and what you can do about improving yourself, both at work and in your personal life. Of course, this book and everything I've learned is based on my own Tortoise journey. Am I the Tortoise who has won the race? Well, I'm still enjoying a good career based on the characteristics and values that have always marked me out as someone who earns his stripes, knuckles down, learns from his mistakes and takes the opportunities when they come. For me, the power of slow, of taking the time to build solid foundations that still support me today, is unbeatable.

While the world needs Hares for their natural talent, charismatic personalities and direct action, it only runs successfully because the far more common Tortoises have stuck it out, through all manner of adversity and challenges, to win through in the end.

If you've made it to the concluding pages of this book, you'll know by now that, it's not possible to *decide* to be a Hare or a Tortoise. By and large, give or take a few hybrids, you're naturally either one or the other. Through these chapters, I hope that you've been able to recognize who you are and that you will go on to capitalize on this new-found knowledge. As much as success is about pushing ourselves forward in the right way, it is also about knowing ourselves – the areas that we naturally excel in and the aspects that we can work on to make the most of ourselves. If you now identify with those Tortoise characteristics and some of those values, it's a great position from which to move forward and make the progress you now realize you can, understanding that you will never be a Hare who crashes and burns.

While I took my time to show you different types of Tortoise, the more you work on your self-development, the more you will combine these different types. If you've been honest enough in the Tortoise Test, you will have identified the areas in which you need to work. Perhaps you've given some of the exercises a try and appreciated how you'll need to practise them over and over again. If you've already been to Tortoise Boot Camp, good on you!

If you've yet to do any of these things, it's time for you to begin making the most of your Tortoise self today. What will it take to nudge you into action? Perhaps recalling something negative that someone has said to you recently at work might give you the initial motivation to improve. Better still, you could try visualizing something incredibly positive. Think about your best life; becoming a superstar at your dream job; the house you'll be living in, the car on the drive; how many people you can make happy through achieving your goals; what a contribution you'll make to the world and how you might change it for the better; how proud of you everyone will be; how proud you'll be of yourself. Use this vision to give you the energy to change. Perhaps it might help you to think of how your life will be if you *don't* put this energy into change. Look at everything you've just imagined. Now, visualize the opposite. Is that a good enough motivator?

Everything I have written about in this book is controllable. That's the most exciting part of maximizing your potential in life – so little of it is down to talent and ability. It's about attitude, work ethic and commitment. Given time, Tortoise characteristics can achieve virtually anything. Understanding and accepting that you are a Tortoise, not a Hare, means that there's less time pressure on you to reach your goals. In no way does this mean that there's no time pressure at all. Urgency and ambition should certainly drive you. Just expect it to take you ten years to build significant momentum.

Don't fret about this. The length of time it takes you to reach the top means more lessons learned, making you better prepared, more able to see the pitfalls, gain special knowledge of the field and relate far more easily to the majority of people on the same trajectory, but who are lower down the ladder.

What's ultimately important is the formation of your values as a professional and a person on the journey. For a Tortoise, the values I've described are the ones that have helped me to maximize my career. I've always tried to live by them. But, as a fallible human being, I've not always succeeded. However, the crucial part is recognizing this as soon as possible and returning to those values. My goal in writing this book is that you develop an understanding of the soft skills it takes to navigate your way through the journey you're on, no matter what stage you're at.

Following the advice I've shared in this book, you'll not only avoid mistakes, but also be seen as advanced for your years and able to handle the many challenges coming your way in a skilled manner that meets the least resistance. The goal is not only success, but longevity.

I wish you the best in making your own luck. Be patient, stay fully committed and you will get there!

ACKNOWLEDGEMENTS

I wanted to thank everyone who has helped me in my own Tortoise journey chronologically, starting with the group of friends that I began playing tennis with in Sutton, particularly Rob Harper and Chris Steers. Our shared love of this great sport led us to watching and playing constantly, and it set my life on a path that I could only have dreamed of back then. Without them, I would not be doing what I'm doing today.

Alongside these friends, I am grateful that the tennis club we played at, Sutton Junior Tennis Centre, was so welcoming to young players and supported me not only in playing there, but also working various jobs at the club, from serving behind the bar to my first job, fitness training tennis players.

I want to sincerely thank each one of the players I've worked with over the years, and those I continue to work with today. I have connected and laughed with them all, and every experience taught me something new.

To my friend Iain Hughes, who has been a constant presence in my life, from coaching me as a kid to working together to being a best man at my wedding. He has taught me the meaning of the word loyalty and has been so much more than a mentor over the years. Thank you.

I also wanted to acknowledge two of the most impactful

characters in my coaching life, Mark Taylor and Leighton Alfred. As I've talked about in this book, Mark gave me my first opportunity in coaching out in Australia before we worked together for five years in Loughborough. It was there that I also met formidable head coach Leighton. My learning curve under their tutelage was almost vertical and it was everything that I needed at that stage in my life and career. I know for a fact that I would not be the coach that I am today without the lessons they taught me.

Of course, I need to thank Andy Murray. The opportunity that he gave me in 2007 and the faith and loyalty that he has shown me since has not only changed mine and my family's life, but has enabled me to realize my dream of working with someone at the very top of their game. He hasn't just shown me the standards required to be the very best in the world, but also the work ethic, sacrifice and uncompromising dedication that I will forever measure myself against. Away from the job, I will always be grateful for his kindness.

I also want to recognize each one of the Team Murray members through the years. We have had so much fun, taught each other so many lessons and I consider each one a true friend.

This book has had its own Tortoise journey. Without the patience and drive of my publishing agent Nick Walters, and the team at David Luxton Associates, it would not have made it onto the shelves. The man who knocked my manuscript into shape and made it readable for you is a talented writer named Mark Griffiths. I vividly remember our first telephone conversation and coming away from it feeling so energized because he immediately understood the tone and message of the book I wanted to write. I enjoyed every minute of our collaboration and I know that he is as proud of this book as I am. A huge debt of gratitude goes to Michael O'Mara Books, and in particular Jo Stansall, for finally turning my dreams into reality. I am truly grateful for all of their support.

When I first began formulating notes into a book, the very first person I shared them with was a close friend of the family, Maxine Ricketts. Aside from being intimidatingly intelligent (she is a magistrate judge), Max has such a wonderfully supportive nature and gave me so much confidence to send my manuscript out to publishers in the first place.

Finally, to my amazing family. No matter where I am in the world, I always know that they are at the end of a telephone and there for me in a heartbeat. My father, David, is my rock in stormy waters and my mother, Janet, is always so positive. They have supported and facilitated every step of my journey and I am so lucky to have them. With the sacrifices I have made to further my career, I haven't always seen enough of them, or my siblings Chris and Joanne, but we remain so close. I am also one of the fortunate few who are blessed with wonderful in-laws. I genuinely look forward to spending time with Jeff and Nicole, and regularly seek their advice when an important decision needs to be made.

I saved these two until last on purpose. The loves of my life – my wife, Vicky, and my son, Oscar. It is a cliché, I know, but every time I put the key in my front door, I am excited and grateful that they are there to welcome me. For years, my wife has dealt with me being away with work, but still manages to be caring and supportive, even when I know she is going through a hard time herself. Without her, I would not have been anywhere near as driven to start the projects that I have. Her wisdom when I am in a difficult situation always seems to hit the mark and she has an uncanny knack of making muddy waters clear. The first time we met, I approached her in a bar and asked her name. '*Je ne parle anglais!*' she replied in broken French. A little defeated, I began to walk away, only to hear her laughing playfully behind me. Ever since, we have filled our house with laughter as often as we can (and she still barely speaks a word of French!).

The origin of this book was slightly morbid. I was spending a long time commuting on the train for work and I wanted to begin writing notes to Oscar that would prepare him for life if, for some reason, I wasn't around anymore. After a few train journeys, these notes started to form pages and pages, and soon a book was born. Ultimately, my son is the motivation behind every single word in these pages. From the minute he was born, he has had to extol every Tortoise value that you will find in this book. He is my inspiration and I dedicate this book to him.

FURTHER READING

For a brilliant guide to managing and engaging with people, in and outside sport:
Conscious Coaching: The Art and Science of Building Buy-in, by Brett Bartholomew, CreateSpace Independent Publishing Platform (2017)

For a classic on the value of living in the present:
The Power of Now: A Guide to Spiritual Enlightenment, by Eckhart Tolle, Yellow Kite (2020)

For an engaging exploration of how our minds work:
The Chimp Paradox: The Mind Management Programme for Confidence, Success and Happiness, by Steve Peters, Vermilion (2012)

For a revealing look at the potential hidden within all of us:
The Secret, by Rhonda Byrne, Simon & Schuster UK (2006)

For an eye-opening book on motivation and the secret to high performance:
Drive: The Surprising Truth About What Motivates Us, by Daniel H. Pink, Canongate (2008)

For a fascinating take on talent and how it can be created and nurtured:
The Talent Code: Greatness Isn't Born. It's Grown, by Daniel Coyle, Arrow (2010)

For Andy's personal story of his incredible journey to become Wimbledon champion:
Seventy-Seven: My Road to Wimbledon Glory, Andy Murray, Headline (2013)

For a revealing look at what really makes a champion:
Bounce: The Myth of Talent and the Power of Practice, by Matthew Syed, HarperCollins (2010)

For insights into creating and shaping talent in sport:
The Talent Lab: The Secret to Finding, Creating and Sustaining Success, by Owen Slot, Ebury (2017)

For an exceptional book on inspirational leadership:
Sevens Heaven: The Beautiful Chaos of Fiji's Olympic Dream, by Ben Ryan, Weidenfeld & Nicolson (2018)

For an authoritative exploration of the important role that emotions play in how we pursue our goals:
Emotional Intelligence: Why It Can Matter More Than IQ, by Daniel Goleman, Bantam (1995)

For a practical account of what it really takes to be a champion:
Legacy: What the All Blacks Can Teach Us About the Business of Life, by James Kerr, Constable (2013)

For a detailed account of Bert Trautmann's extraordinary determination:
Trautmann's Journey: From Hitler Youth to FA Cup Legend, by Catrine Clay, Yellow Jersey (2010)

For the inside track on what makes a humble champion tick:
Rafa: My Story, by Rafael Nadal, Sphere (2011)

For a must-read on organizing your thoughts, priorities and goals:
Clarity: Clear Mind, Better Performance, Bigger Results, by Jamie Smart, Capstone (2013)

For a leading psychologist's account of how we can motivate ourselves and others with the right mindset:
Mindset: Changing the Way You Think to Fulfil Your Potential, Carol Dweck, Robinson (2012)

INDEX

BUTTERFLIES
you give me

welcome
sweet little baby